Dr. Baloian and Dr. Hartley
College professors who expand minds, stir hearts,
and model faith—
Preparing us all for postcollege life.

I have studied many times
    The marble which was chiseled for me—
    A boat with a furled sail at rest in a harbor.
    In truth it pictures not my destination
    But my life.
    For love was offered me and I shrank from its disillusionment;
    Sorrow knocked at my door, but I was afraid;
    Ambition called to me, but I dreaded the chances.
    And now I know that we must lift the sail
    And catch the winds of destiny
    Wherever they drive the boat.
    To put meaning in one's life may end in madness,
    But life without meaning is the torture
    Of restlessness and vague desire—
    It is a boat longing for the sea and yet afraid.

Edgar Lee Masters, "George Gray,"
Spoon River Anthology

Contents

Introduction:
Why Prepare for Postcollege Life?

Ten Years After

Out of the blue, Jim called. We'd gone to college together, been roommates. We reminisced about the old days and played the "whatever-happened-to-so-and-so?" game.

"By the way, what about Nick?" I asked.

"I think he's working at a shoe store in Long Beach."

"You're kidding! Working at a shoe store? You're pulling my leg." (Jim was the joker in our crowd.) "Come on, Jim, seriously, what's Nick doing?"

"Well, Sam called and told me that Nick was working at a discount shoe store." It had been seven years since I had last seen Nick. At that time he was what I would have called a *spiritual giant* on campus, a natural leader. He sponsored mission trips to Mexico, held Bible studies in his off-campus apartment. He was the president of the big Christian club on campus and had a vital, active ministry. For sure, I thought he would be pastoring a big church by now, heading up some dynamic ministry or serving as a missionary in some exotic place. How could Nick, with all his education and leadership abilities, end up selling discount shoes at a Long Beach mall?

"What happened?" I asked, still unbelieving.

"I heard he'd had some bad times. Judy left him after a year of marriage. I'm not sure of the details but I doubt if he even goes to church anymore."

Now I *was* depressed. Floored. My last image of Nick was of a handsome, athletic young man, holding a leather-bound Bible while he conducted an evening devotion for about fifty students at a little mission on the Baja peninsula in Mexico. The students were captivated by his charisma. He was bright, a compelling speaker and had a tremendous grasp of the Scriptures. He was *very* convincing and passionate about his beliefs.

1

Jim went on to fill in the disheartening details. "Nick's life took a downward spiral once he left campus. After he graduated and relinquished his various leadership roles, his faith seemed to wither and dry up. It's weird isn't it? Sad, really."

Jim and I concluded our call, trying to be cheery, sharing family news and promising to call again, soon—and we'd pray for Nick—but I just couldn't shake the strange and terrible news I had just heard. What had happened? How does someone go from being a dynamic instrument of God, used to touch hundreds of university students, to a person who just gives up on his faith? My questions kept coming. Was his faith experience in college real or just a façade? Did a few bad decisions or tragedies permanently derail his spiritual life? Could faith be just a temporary mask or something like trendy jeans that get discarded when they're no longer in style? Jim's news about Nick was troubling, but the issues his news raised were even more troubling.

Unfortunately, Nick's story is not unique. Over the years I have seen too many dynamic, faith-filled collegians graduate, only to see their faith slowly lose relevance as they moved into their careers. They are like flames starved of oxygen, slowly losing their intensity, their heat, and their passion.

But, happily, I have witnessed the lives of other students whose faith has steadily strengthened since their college days. Their commitments have deepened. Their influence for God's work in their communities has increased. Their spirituality has become increasingly part of their vocations and careers. Rather than fizzling after a college faith experience, those students continued to build on the behaviors and habits that were initiated during their undergraduate years.

But what makes the difference? Why is a college faith experience for some like that of a hothouse plant? In a controlled environment, the plant flourishes and blossoms. But when the same plant meets the hostile summer weather in a garden, too often that plant does not withstand the radical change—much to the gardener's dismay. Exposed to the elements, the plant withers.

But then there is another group of students. For them the college faith experience provides the sun and nutrients that establish deep roots, ensuring long-term growth. When *they* meet the hostile realities, they flourish. Is it strength of character? Fate? Genetics? Darwin's "only the strong survive"? Or is it a matter of preparation? How does a person develop behav-

If Jesus Were a Senior

Last-Minute Preparations for Postcollege Life

Bruce Main

Westminster John Knox Press
LOUISVILLE • LONDON

Scripture quotations, unless otherwise indicated, are from the New Revised Standard Version of the Bible, copyright © 1989 by the Division of Christian Education of the National Council of the Churches of Christ in the U.S.A., and used by permission.

Scripture quotations marked NEB are taken from *The New English Bible,* © The Delegates of the Oxford University Press and The Syndics of the Cambridge University Press, 1961, 1970. Used by permission.

Scripture marked NIV is taken from the Holy Bible, New International Version®. Copyright © 1973, 1978, 1984 by International Bible Society. Used by permission of Zondervan Publishing House. All rights reserved.

Excerpts from Martin Luther King Jr.'s "I Have a Dream" speech and quotations from his book *Why We Can't Wait* are reprinted by arrangement with the Estate of Martin Luther King Jr., c/o Writers House as agent for the proprietor, New York, NY. Copyright 1963 Martin Luther King Jr., copyright renewed 1991 Coretta Scott King.

Where so indicated, scripture is taken from The Message. Copyright © by Eugene H. Peterson, 1993, 1994, 1995. Used by permission of NavPress Publishing Group.

Book design by Sharon Adams
Cover design by Jennifer K. Cox

First edition
Published by Westminster John Knox Press
Louisville, Kentucky

This book is printed on acid-free paper that meets the American National Standards Institute Z39.48 standard. ∞

PRINTED IN THE UNITED STATES OF AMERICA

03 04 05 06 07 08 09 10 11 12 — 10 9 8 7 6 5 4 3 2 1

Library of Congress Cataloging-in-Publication Data

Main, Bruce,
    If Jesus were a senior : preparations for postcollege discipleship /
    by Bruce Main.—1st ed.
       p. cm.
    Includes bibliographical references.
    ISBN 0-664-22566-7 (alk. paper)
      1. College students—Religious life. 2. College graduates—
    Religious life. I. Title.

BV45313 .M35 2003
248.8'34—dc21   2002028058

iors and disciplines during one's college years that ensure continued growth and a deepening faith?

Preparations for the Journey

Annie Dillard writes in *Teaching A Stone to Talk: Expeditions and
Encounters* that in 1845 Sir John Franklin and 138 officers left
England to find the Canadian Arctic's northwest passage to the
Pacific Ocean. Dillard describes each sailing vessel carrying an
auxiliary steam engine and a twelve-day emergency supply of
coal for the two-year voyage. Instead of wisely carrying additional coal, each ship made room for a 1,200-volume library, a
hand organ that could play fifty tunes, china place settings, cut-
glass wine goblets, and sterling silver flatware—no ordinary silver, but an ornate Victorian design with heavy, richly patterned
handles. And, to add to the absurdity, the expedition carried no
special clothing for the Arctic—only the fancy uniforms of Her
Majesty's navy.

Sir John Franklin and his crew did not complete the journey.
The sailing vessels were caught in the ice, and the men died.
Later, when another exploratory group discovered some of the
frozen bodies, they found the place settings engraved with each
officer's initials and family crests. Other bodies were found in
uniforms "of fine blue cloth . . . edged with silk braid, with
sleeves slashed and bearing five covered buttons each."[1]

Yes, inadequate and inappropriate preparations were made
for Franklin's journey. Those who planned the trip had no clue
about the cruelty and harshness of the terrain and environment.
As they made their plans, they were not willing to make the sacrifices and take what was *really* needed for the trip. In the midst
of the hype and excitement of becoming famous explorers,
blinded by their enlarged sense of self, they lost awareness of
their own mortality. They naively did not respect the power of
nature or the customs of those who lived and survived in the
harsh climates they were entering. After all, they were British—
citizens of the most powerful country in the world. Libraries
and fancy clothing were regarded as more vital than additional
fuel. It was more important to *look good* in sharp uniforms than
to humble themselves and adopt the clothing of Arctic climates.
Theirs was a poorly planned journey.

Life after college can be likened to Franklin's expedition
through the Arctic. The world can be an unfriendly place. In
fact—and this may come as a surprise for young graduates eager

for a job—the workplace can be downright hostile. I recently asked a young college graduate what she had learned in her first year of work. She said, with impressive anguish, "I never knew that people could be so evil." She had been bruised by office politics and had witnessed backstabbing and intentional character defamation—just so that certain individuals could advance their status and move up the success ladder.

Will a good GPA and strong graduate school recommendations really help as a person tries to hold on to his or her integrity in a workplace, rather than compromise by overlooking company wrongdoings or the unethical behavior of coworkers? What will you do when your new job requires all your best life energy and does not allow time for your personal development and relationships? How will you balance the demands of family, work, and Christian service? Or, if you are financially successful, how will you respond to the seductions of money and power? Will your faith influence the way you make your decisions?

Those are some of the tough questions you will face. Academic performance, the name of your alma mater, or your awards will help little. Unless you go deeper, your Christian witness will lose its vibrancy and passion, and your faith will become compartmentalized, relegated to some far corner of your existence.

Finding answers for this part of the journey begins with how you "pack" for the expedition. Packing will require a careful and wise use of the last few years of your young adulthood, so that the right ideas, disciplines, habits, and guiding principles will be a natural, God-given part of your life.

"Quarterlife" Crisis

The many decisions that need to be made immediately following graduation can also make early adulthood a very confusing time of life. Alexandra Robbins and Abby Wilner recently published an interesting book titled *Quarterlife Crisis: The Unique Challenges of Life in Your Twenties.* Robbins and Wilner argue that much attention has been given to midlife crisis, and to the struggles of adolescence, but very little attention has been given to the crisis "twentysomethings" face upon graduation. Through interviews with more than a hundred twentysomethings, the authors come to an important conclusion: postcollege years, often thought of as "the best years of our lives," can be years of intense personal crisis, depression, and a deep sense of loss. The worst aspect of this dilemma, claim Robbins and

Wilner, is that twentysomethings have few places to go for help. They cannot afford therapy (unlike their midlife counterparts who often have resources), and there are few real outlets in our present society where young adults can work through these issues. To support their claim, Robbins and Wilner note the profound absence of academic research and professional services specifically devoted to this period of life.

Why does this quarterlife crisis exist? The core reason for a quarterlife crisis is that this period—more than most periods in our lives—is marked by extreme change and transition. "After about twenty years in a sheltered school setting," write the authors, "—or more if a person has gone on to graduate or professional school—many graduates undergo some sort of culture shock. In the academic environment, goals were clear-cut and the ways to achieve them were mapped out distinctly."[2] Transitioning out of twenty years of structured life can create a serious crisis of self-identity and meaning. For all of their conscious life, their academic accomplishments, the college they attend, or the undergraduate study program to which they have committed has defined the twentysomething student. The authors suggest,

"But after graduation, the pathways blur. In that crazy, wild nexus that people like to call the 'real world,' there is no definitive way to get from point A to point B, regardless of whether the points are related to a career, financial situation, home, or social life . . . the extreme uncertainty that twentysomethings experience after graduation occurs because what was once a solid line that they could follow throughout their series of educational institutions has now disintegrated into millions of different options."[3] Many think that these "millions of different options" can provide a sense of hope and unlimited opportunity. But the authors remind us that "the endless array of decisions can also make a recent graduate feel utterly lost."[4]

Not all twentysomethings experience this crisis. Many college graduates do transition smoothly and find their place and calling in this world. The research of Robbins and Wilner suggests, however, that it is normal for graduates to struggle and to realize that they are not alone in their struggle. Thousands of others are experiencing the same frustrations, fears, and confusion.

Unfortunately, Robbins and Wilner's book falls short in helping students discover their true identity and find their vocation. It is interesting and disheartening that the book devotes only one page to discussing the significance of faith and faith communities in young adult decision making. Perhaps the reason so many of the interviewees struggled so intensely with feelings of despair and angst is that faith was *not* part of their lives. These students had a profound void in their lives, which intensified their twentysomething struggle. Issues of identity and vocation are directly connected to a person's faith and worldview.

I remember very vividly sitting in the bleachers of my university's football stadium one afternoon during the spring semester of my senior year. As I looked up at the Azusa foothills, I realized that I needed to make some major decisions—I could not delay any longer. Should I look for a full-time job? Should I go to graduate school? If so, which school? Should I go work for a mission organization on the east coast, or should I continue to serve with a ministry on the west coast? What was God's will for my life? How was I supposed to find that will? All these decisions began to really hit that afternoon, and I began to feel anxious. There were too many choices.

But, I can honestly say, my faith commitment played a major role in influencing and guiding the decisions I needed to make. Yes, there were moments of intense doubt, moments of fear, and moments of confusion—major life decisions are never easy! Yet in the midst of the searching and seeking, I found myself unearthing guidance and direction from the events, ideas, and convictions that I had developed during my university years. Mentoring relationships I had built with professors became key to seeking wisdom. Values and life goals I had solidified during the previous four years gave me a sense of "centeredness" that helped my thinking and decision-making process. Events, service opportunities, and mission trips in which I had participated during my college years provided valuable insights into my passions and gifts. And I believed that God would guide my searching. All these "precrisis" *preparations* helped tremendously as I struggled to make wise decisions.

Over the years I have had the privilege of watching hundreds of college and university graduates come through the ministry of UrbanPromise. These graduates come and spend a year or two serving children and teens in the inner city of Camden, New Jersey; Wilmington, Delaware; Toronto, Ontario; or Vancouver, British Columbia.[5] They are incredible young men and women who love with passion overlooked and forgotten youth of the United States and Canada. I am blessed to be in their presence. Many of these students come to the inner city because they sense a calling from God. Other students make this commitment because they are searching for direction and trying to find God's will for their lives. I have made a few observations, of which one in particular stands out: regardless of motivation, those young adults whose twentysomething years are most fruitful, most creative, and most filled with opportunities to grow in their faith are usually students who have *prepared well* during their college years. These are students who before graduation have reflected on the implications of their faith, have learned to serve sacrificially, have tried to discern God's calling for their life, and have begun to cultivate a dream that calls them into God's redemptive plan for the world. Good *preparation* makes a difference.

If Jesus Were a Senior

I believe in the humanity of Jesus as much as I believe in his divinity. Too often Christians elevate the divinity of Jesus and make him to be some sort of cosmic Superman who just floats down to earth at the age of thirty and begins a dynamic three-year ministry. Those unthinking Christians focus on the things that make Jesus different—his miracles, his healings, and his sacrificial death. They forget the things Jesus had in common with us—childhood and adolescence, family, friends, relationships, satisfactions and disappointments.

I do not want to belittle or downplay the importance of the final weeks of Jesus' life and ministry. But focusing *only* on that aspect of his life denies the community of believers access to the other attributes of God's revelation to us: God's heart, God's grace, God's love, and God's intention for how humans should live, as demonstrated by the day-to-day life of Jesus. Likewise, if we focus only on the postresurrection Jesus, we get a truncated, incomplete picture of God's *good news* message to humanity. We meet a Jesus who is not connected to real people who live real lives, deal with real issues, and face real struggles. That Jesus has little to say to people who desire to live a more authentic and God-centered life. As well, that Jesus has little to say to young adults who are trying to figure out how to discover what it means to be truly Christian in a complex and hostile world.

But a vibrant, human Jesus speaks and encourages me in another way: I realize that he had to make choices—not just choices between sin and obedience, but normal, everyday choices. Jesus had to decide with whom he would spend his time, whether he would pray or take a nap, study the Torah or go out and play. He had to decide whether he would follow in his human father's footsteps and become a carpenter or do something else with his life. Unfortunately, other than Luke's reference that the boy Jesus "grew in wisdom and stature" (2:52 NIV), the Scriptures are largely silent about the years leading up to Jesus' ministry. But I do not think it is erroneous or heretical, just because the Scriptures are silent, to assume that his life decisions made prior to his thirtieth year influenced his ministry. For example, Jesus knew and understood people, he was an effective communicator through his stories and the metaphors of his day, and he captivated the imagination with God's truth. Jesus understood the Old Testament Scriptures—suggesting he had developed a discipline for study. He certainly had the discipline of prayer.

I do not believe that Jesus was *just* mystically endowed with these attributes and gifts. I do not believe that Jesus grew up in a cultural and spiritual vacuum and that, at the age of thirty, the Holy Spirit just breathed these attributes into his psyche. Rather, Jesus cultivated these habits and disciplines in the years leading to his full-time ministry. Jesus "*grew* in stature and wisdom."

How would Jesus spend his final years of college? Is it too far-fetched to raise this hypothetical question? I don't think so. Why? Because Jesus was a real person. He was once twenty-three. He celebrated a twenty-fourth birthday in some way traditional for his Middle Eastern, Hebrew culture. He lived past his twenty-fifth year. Certainly he did not go through the pressures of final exams and graduation ceremonies, but he vigorously and joyously participated in his early adulthood.

So how would Jesus spend *his* critical young adult years? Since he was preparing for a life of ministry, what would be his commitments during those years? How would he spend his time? What would be his priorities? What would he "pack" for the journey? Of course, this side of heaven we will never know the answers to these questions. But what we can know is that everyone's life is a gift. The struggles and the questions unique to us are important and part of our individual, wonderful journey. The question then becomes, How would Jesus want someone who chooses to live a life as God's faithful witness to spend these important years so he or she can be prepared for a long life of faithful discipleship?

In these next chapters I will offer some ideas and suggestions for how you, a young adult, might use your final years of college in preparation for the radical changes of life in *the real world*. And further, I will attempt to challenge you to develop a series of preparations that will help guide you in living a life of *faithful discipleship*.

A Conversation with Jesus

A person will miss many events and activities after college: friends, football games, late night conversations. Standing in lines to purchase books at the beginning of each semester is not one of those events. I still have nightmares of juggling seventy-five pounds of hardcover textbooks—with a $312 price tag!—only to find when I get to the cash register that the class I need to graduate is full. I am sure you can relate to this experience.

I wonder what Jesus might say to each of us if he caught us unexpectedly at the beginning of our final year of university. I can imagine this scene.

"This is it!" comes a Voice from behind me.

I keep my eyes focused on the cashier, who is now only twelve bodies away from me. I am determined not to lose my space, not to be distracted. Why the bookstore will not hire another part-time cashier at the beginning of each semester, I will never know.

"What do you mean?" I reply.

"This is your last year. Then you'll be out in the real world," continues the Visitor. "Will you be ready?"

I never really liked people who use the term real world. *The term assumes that college is* not *real. It sure feels real to me. The last thing on my mind is life after graduation. That idea seems like an eternity away. I just want to buy my books without bouncing a check and survive my senior thesis. My Friend decides to offer more advice.*

"Use this year wisely. Prepare well. Be diligent. It will make a difference in how you live your life."

"I am planning on studying hard," I respond. "You know, I need a good GPA if I am going to get into a good graduate program."

"How do you know I want you to go to graduate school?" comes the reply. "Are you sure this is God's intention for your life?"

I realize now who is talking. I am about to respond, but He continues.

"I'm not just talking about studying hard. Sure, that's part of the process, but I need you to make preparations of faith that will help you

navigate your way through a very complex and difficult world. Academics are only a small piece of a much bigger picture."

Up until this point I had not really thought much about life beyond the following May. But my Friend had a point—an important point. What was going to define me after I graduated? How would my faith influence my career decisions? How would I begin to prepare for the journey of Christian discipleship in a hostile world? These were important questions—questions that needed time and attention.

But then I heard a voice.

"Mister, will that be cash, check, or charge?"

Then I realized that the journey had started.

Remember:

My first conversion, if you want to call it that, was a life-changing thing. So were my subsequent new beginnings. But life doesn't stop. And I've come to realize that if I am going to live authentically, I must continually go through new cycles of repentance and renewal. I look forward to those times because that's when I'm most alive.

Johann Christoph Arnold

Reflections for Students

1. What do you hope your faith will look like in ten years? How do you hope your faith will be integrated into your life? Your career? Your family?

2. What are you presently "packing" for the journey? What practical steps are you taking to prepare for life after college?

3. Who are some adult Christian role models you admire? Why do you admire the way they live out their faith? What did these role models "pack for the journey" during their college years?

4. How do you think Jesus wants you to use your last years of university?

For the Leader

Have your students imagine that they are packing a suitcase for a life journey. Ask them to make a list of the attributes, disciplines, and behaviors that they would like to pack in that bag. After they have completed this list, have the students discuss how they can prepare now to develop these behaviors.

Meditation

Lord,

Thanks for this incredible period of life.
Thanks for opportunities to study, to meet new people,
    and to grow.
Thanks for a sense of future.

Guide my decisions in the coming months.
Awake my mind to see what preparations I need to make
    for the journey.
Stir my heart to consider wise decisions I need to make.

May my preparations provide a foundation on which I can build
        a life of faithfulness,
        a life of compassion,
        a life of love,
        a life of vision,
        and a life of calling.

Provide the discipline, the patience, and the courage to prepare
    well for my postcollege life.

Amen

Chapter 1

Dream Preparations:
Participating in God's Drama

It is rather to say that those who dream no dreams shall have no visions; this poverty is not virtue; this poverty is the worst kind of impoverishment—the lack and fear of imagination.

Peter J. Gomes

Imperative Dreams

Recently I gave a series of talks at a youth retreat to a group of inner-city teens. They were exceptional young people who had overcome incredible obstacles to get to where they were. Each had lived in one of the most economically depressed cities in America—a city with few opportunities, an abysmal educational system, poverty, and drugs. Yet they still had a sparkle in their eyes. Their community had not beaten them down nor gotten the better of them. They still had their dreams.

I really wanted my talks to connect with those young people, for too often speakers miss their audiences when speaking to adolescents. They talk too long, are condescending, speak over everyone's heads, or fail to be relevant. I wanted these young people to walk away from the retreat with a sense of hope and a desire to fight against all the negative forces working against them.

I began my talk by saying that there is a Bible verse chiseled on the grave marker of Martin Luther King Jr. I looked intently at the crowd of young people. "It reads like this," I said, "Here comes this dreamer. Come now, let us kill him . . . and we shall see what will become of his dreams. Genesis 37:19–20." Since the students seemed less than enthusiastic about these obscure verses, I urged them to repeat the verse with me. They began to wake up.

"Here comes this dreamer. Come now, let us kill him . . . and we shall see what will become of his dreams. Genesis 37:19–20," they chanted in unison.

"Say it again! This time *with feeling*."

"Here comes this dreamer. Come now, let us kill him . . . and we shall see what will become of his dreams. Genesis 37:19–20," they screamed. The group was now involved. I could feel the energy level in the room begin to rise. I knew I had their attention.

I went on to explain to my newly energized audience that the verse we had been reciting was about a young man in the Bible named Joseph. "Joseph was your age and had been given a dream by God. And it was *a remarkable dream*. Yet when the younger brother Joseph shared his dream with his older brothers," I was moving now, "they became jealous and resentful. They decided they would kill him. They beat him up and left him in the ditch to die! *They tried to kill the dreamer*. They thought they would get rid of both the dream *and* the dreamer."

Impulsively I decided to do something a little different.

"Cassandra!" I yelled. "Come sit in one of the chairs beside me. These are my dream chairs."

Slowly and sheepishly Cassandra made her way to the front of the auditorium. In her personal life she had overcome incredible adversity. Her health was poor. Her family life had been chaotic and dysfunctional. She had seen relatives and friends die in the drug wars. But *she had not given up*. She had a dream. She was a dreamer. Not only was she the first in her family to go to college, but she had also been awarded a full scholarship.

"Cassandra is a dreamer," I reminded the crowd. "God gave her a dream, a dream to go to college, to become a social worker, and to return to the broken inner city and work with teens who need help."

The auditorium erupted in applause. The younger teens applauded with respect. They cheered with admiration.

"But it wasn't easy for Cassandra," I continued. "Everything around her tried to kill her dream—her family, her health, events in her community. But she persevered." The young people in the auditorium continued to cheer wildly.

"Edy, come on up here and sit in one of my dream chairs," I motioned to a young man sitting to my right. Edy began to make his way to the stage. As he walked down the isle the kids began to chant his name. "Ed-y, Ed-y."

Edy had grown up in the housing projects on the east side of town. His mother still battles cancer. He never knew his father. His uncle was a big-time drug dealer. Edy should have been in jail or dead—as things can go in tough communities—but Edy was about to enter his first year of college. In a school system that sees 60 percent of its students drop out of high school before their senior year and fewer than 5 percent of those who do finish go on and graduate from college, the fact that Edy had graduated from high school was more than a miracle.

"Edy is a dreamer," I continued. I was psyched. "God gave Edy a dream to go to college. He's starting this September. He wants to get an education so he can give back his skills to his community. Let's give him a big hand."

By this time the audience was with me. They were cheering. They were shouting. They were encouraging Edy.

For the next fifteen minutes I pulled four more "dreamers" out of the crowd. Each student had overcome tremendous obstacles. But despite their trials, they had held on to the dreams God had given them. *Nothing was going to kill their dream.*

I went on to tell the teens that God wanted to give *each of them* a dream for their life. Then in a sober note I also cautioned them that everything around them would try to kill the dream that God had given them. I reminded them that, like Joseph, they might find that those most resistant to their dream would be their own family.

As I ended my talk, I sensed that the youth had been challenged and encouraged. Recognizing that in our midst there were dreamers who had overcome great adversities, I prayed that my message would be one they would never forget.

When I was walking toward the back of the auditorium to go to my cabin for the night, I heard a young voice call my name. I turned around and was greeted by a fourteen-year-old Vietnamese girl named Lyn. Her parents were Buddhists, but she had gotten involved with our ministry and had made a commitment to Christ. "Mr. Bruce," she began. "I just want you to know that I hope to be in the dream chair one day. I want God to give me my dream." She went on to tell me that she had struggled with depression and had even had some thoughts of suicide. But now she was going to make it to the dream chair. Then she would not let anything kill the dream that God would give her.

I was deeply moved by her comments. As I looked into her eyes, I could sense her sincerity—yes, Lyn would sit in one of the dream chairs. How did I know? Because I have witnessed over the years that young people who *make it* in the inner city are young people who have a dream. Only youth with a dream can withstand the relentless wave of destructive forces. Without a dream, kids become lost; but with a dream, young people are able to rise above the hopelessness and deplorable conditions of their environment. You see, dreams provide *hope*. Dreams provide a *sense of future*. Dreams give *direction*. Dreams supply *courage* in the midst of adversity. Without dreams people are lost. Without dreams people—not just inner-city kids—succumb to evil and the status quo as though it were normal. We are created to dream!

Joseph the Dreamer

The biblical story of Joseph is a remarkable testimony to the power of a dream. It is Joseph's dream that guides him and sustains him during very difficult times. But ultimately his dream reminds him of his place and role in a much bigger drama—not a drama of rejection and failure, but a drama orchestrated by God.

Any reader of Joseph's story (starting in Genesis 37) quickly learns that Joseph was a unique and special young man. He was his father's favorite, handsome, and the youngest of the family. I am sure that his attributes were enough to elicit a few black eyes from his older brothers—sibling rivalry at its finest. Then, to make family matters worse, Joseph announced that he had had *a dream*! You just know that caught the family's attention. But when he told the dream to his family there was—let's say it kindly—a strongly negative reaction. With vivid and less-than-subtle imagery Joseph announced that he would one day rule over his brothers. Not only would Joseph rule over his brothers and his mother and father, but they would all bow down and revere him as their Lord! Pretty tough talk for a kid of seventeen.

Not surprisingly, the dream created a violent reaction within the family. The result: the brothers beat him, sold him as a slave to some traveling merchants, and then convinced their father that his favorite son had been killed. "See, here's the blood to prove it!" The terrible story has all the makings of a Hollywood movie—envy, violence, cover-ups, and lies.

But one has to wonder what was going on in Joseph's mind as he was strapped to a camel and taken into Egyptian slavery. One minute he was his father's favorite, with a remarkable vision for his life; a few minutes later he was a forgotten nobody with no family, no friends, and no control over his destiny. I am sure this was not the career path Joseph imagined would take him towards lordship. But he did have a dream. And his dream gave him the strength to persevere, to triumph, to win.

Well—you probably know the story—upon arriving in Egypt things began to look up for Joseph. Although he was in a new country, surrounded by new people, and confronting the challenges associated with transitioning to a new culture, Joseph succeeded very well. As a matter of fact, the Lord was with Joseph, and quickly Joseph was given tremendous responsibility within the household of one of Pharaoh's officials named Potiphar. Potiphar realized "that the LORD was with him and that the LORD caused all that he did to prosper in his hands" (Gen. 39:3–4). Potiphar put him in charge of everything.

But then the first real test was thrown at Joseph. Potiphar's wife noticed this well-built, handsome, self-assured, and competent young man strolling around the palace, and she tried to seduce him. Day after day she tried to get young Joseph into her grasp. But Joseph remained strong and did not give into her relentless advances. With his boss away and tempting sex dangled in front of him, Joseph withstood the allures of a powerful woman—a woman who was used to getting whatever she wanted, and she wanted Joseph.

How did Joseph withstand the temptation? Did he have a low sex drive? Did Potiphar's wife not turn him on? Old Testament scholar Walter Brueggemann argues that it is deeper than those reasons. He contends that Joseph was a man of deep passion but could withstand the seduction because he was a man of destiny—he had a "destiny not to be squandered on a fling of passion." Brueggemann further claims "it is *the dream* that makes this man, and that woman cannot take it from him."[6] When a person has a dream—a sense of divine destiny—he or she has something to focus upon when temporal distractions are thrown their way. Joseph was not derailed, because he held to his dream. His purpose, deeply imbedded within his heart and subconscious, was to please God first.

But, as the story unfolds, Joseph was not rewarded for his fidelity and faithfulness to God. Rather, Joseph was framed by Potiphar's wife and thrown in prison for two years. One wonders what was going through Joseph's mind. Ending up in prison does not seem to be leading him closer to the fulfillment of his dream. Once again, Joseph was powerless, shamed, and alone. His life was out of his control. He was vulnerable and totally at the mercy of God. Yet we read that when Joseph was in the bowels of an Egyptian prison, "the LORD was with Joseph" (Gen. 39:21). Even though Joseph's career path certainly was not on a linear projectile, Joseph was given glimpses that the Lord was still present and active.

I don't know about you, but to me two years in prison seems like a long time—especially during the prime of one's life. What gave Joseph the hope to hang on during those years of imprisonment? What gave Joseph the confidence not to give up during those dark hours of aloneness? I have to believe that it was his sense of destiny—*the dream* that God had given him for his life. Dreams provide *hope*. Dreams provide *a sense of future*. Dreams give us the courage *to hold* on during the difficult times. Dreams provide *the focus* our lives need so we can maintain a moral vision. Joseph had a dream.

The end of the Joseph story is remarkable. Joseph eventually was released from prison and became Pharaoh's right-hand man because of his God-given ability to interpret dreams. He saved the Egyptian empire from total starvation and ruin, and saved his family—the people of Israel—from extinction. And yes, Joseph's brothers did bow down and honor their youngest brother. The dream was fulfilled. Joseph, the man of divine destiny, was able to withstand the trials and temptations and maintain his faithfulness to God. Because of Joseph's unwillingness to give up, his refusal to take shortcuts, and his unwillingness to become seduced by his personal achievement and personal success, God's purposes were fulfilled. Could this have happened without a dream? Without a stubborn belief that he was part of God's larger drama? I doubt it. Dreams are critical.

Tell Them about the Dream

Certainly Joseph was not the only person in history with a dream and a divine sense of destiny. One of the recent dreamers in our history was Martin Luther King Jr. Besides being remembered for his tremendous civil rights work, King has been immortalized for his "I have a dream" speech given on August 28, 1963, on the steps of the Lincoln Memorial in Washington, D.C. As he was nearing the conclusion of his prepared remarks on that great sunny day, the gospel singer Mahalia Jackson, who was sitting close by the stage, shouted out: "Tell them about the dream!"[7] For the next five minutes King extemporaneously planted a dream in the hearts and minds of us all.

So I say to you, my friends,
that even though we must face the difficulties
    of today and tomorrow,
I still have a dream.
It is a dream deeply rooted in the American dream
that one day this nation will rise up and live out
    the true meaning of its creed
—we hold these truths to be self-evident,
    that all men are created equal.

I have a dream that one day on the red hills of Georgia,
sons of former slaves and sons of former slave-owners
will be able to sit down together at the table
    of brotherhood.[8]

King continued to paint a picture of the dream for his audience by claiming "I have a dream that my four little children will one day live in a nation where they will not be judged by the color of their skin but by the content of their character. *I have a dream today!*"

Why is his speech remembered and quoted so often? Because it speaks of a dream. The speech did not articulate a plan, a strategy, or a series of goals. It did not articulate a mission statement for the civil rights movement, nor did it communicate a vision. King spoke of dreams. The speech painted an image for the country—an image of what the country could become. King connected with every human being who had ears to hear. He connected because every human being has had dreams—or needs one.

I believe it was his dream that kept King motivated when things were bleak. His vivid image of a country where people would be judged not by the color of their skin but by the content of their character kept King hopeful, even in the midst of depressing circumstances. What gave those who fought so hard for civil rights the courage to continue? King's dream gave people the persistence to endure the Montgomery bus boycott. His dream gave people the stubborn will not to back down from fire hoses and police dogs. His dream gave the Freedom Riders and those who picketed segregated lunch counters the will and determination not to give up. His dream gave people the hope that their efforts to register voters would make a difference. Dreams *are* powerful. Dreams have the ability to take ordinary people beyond their limitations and to help them do remarkable things with their lives.

Finding a Dream: Mentors

How does a young adult, perhaps a college senior, find a life dream? How does a person uncover a kind of divine destiny that will give guidance and clarity to a life? Here are a few ideas that I have found helpful.

Mentors are essential to help you find your dream or affirm the dream you already have. Unfortunately, in our university system, it has become increasingly difficult for students to build relationships with a faculty member or an older adult who can affirm and encourage their dream. Daniel Levinson, in his classic book *The Seasons of a Man's Life*, suggests that the true mentor "fosters the young adult's development by believing in him, sharing the youthful Dream and giving it his blessing." Levinson continues by claiming that "the mentor has another function, and this is developmentally the most crucial one: to support and facilitate the *realization* of the Dream."[9] Levinson argues convincingly that this adult endorsement, this adult blessing of the dream, is a critical piece in helping the student move toward fulfilling his or her dream.

One of the benefits of a small college is the opportunity to get to know faculty. Classes of ten to twenty students often allow unique opportunities to build relationships with professors and meet potential mentors. That was true in my life. Prior to college I never even considered the idea of becoming a minister. I enrolled as a business major my freshman year. I soon changed to an English major. Later, after taking some really great theology and religion classes, I decided to make another shift and declared a major in theology. That started me on my road toward ministry. But it was not the content of the theology courses that persuaded me to make another change in my major. What drove me to make changes were the professors. They were men and women whom I wanted to be around and be like. They were people who took a personal interest in my vocational choices and me.

One professor especially had a tremendous impact on many students. He was different. What made Professor Bruce Baloian different? I'm convinced it was that he actually wanted to get to know his students. *Students* were the reason he had become a teacher. Students and the careers of students were placed above his personal ambitions. Rather than limiting his office hours so he could write books and do research, Professor

Baloian contrived creative ways to get students into his office so he could meet them on a personal basis. Before embarking on a new writing assignment or term paper, students had to book appointments in his office to discuss the topic. That was Professor Baloian's way of keeping his fingers on the pulse of campus life and developing mentoring relationships with his students. It was no accident that his classes were always the largest on campus. Students knew that he cared. As an adult and parent, I now realize that the hours of personal time he spent with students were a tremendous sacrifice for both his career and family.

But I could never get an A in Professor Baloian's classes. A few Bs, sure, and even once an A–. But his tests were difficult and he demanded a great deal of study. He graded all our papers *personally*—very few students received A's. If you wanted to score well, to keep your GPA at a high level, his were not the classes to take. I remember his returning a fifteen-page paper of mine with a B written on the top in red felt pen. I had worked hard on the paper. My facial expression was one of great disappointment. But he gave me a smile and shared some words that I will never forget. "The best ministers are usually the B students," he said with encouragement. That was the ringing endorsement I needed to hear. It was enough to make me ponder the possibility; maybe, just maybe, I had the stuff to do ministry.

Then, further, Professor Baloian opened the doors for my first youth ministry. He had heard about a need at a local high school for an outreach worker and he recommended me for the job. To have *his* endorsement was a tremendous boost to my flagging self-confidence.

Professor Baloian's encouragement got me to take the job. So when I had to raise personal support for my salary, it was Professor Baloian who faithfully contributed a monthly check of $80 to help offset my costs—and I was not the only former student he supported. When I could not afford a place to stay on my meager salary, Professor Baloian set up a cot in his son's room. When I had ministry-related questions, he would *make time* to share his advice. Professor Baloian went far beyond what was required on him. He was a true mentor.

Beyond that, one of the greatest gifts Professor Baloian gave to students were stories. He *loved* to tell stories. His stories inspired his students, especially those who were developing an interest and calling toward ministry. His stories painted pictures—gave us images—of what could be. Twenty years earlier, he told us, he had done youth outreach ministry. So his stories connected to my heart and fueled my own dream to reach youth. His stories made me believe that great things could be done through those who served God. The endorsement of a mentor was critical to the formation of *my dreams*. Professor Baloian's *blessing* was absolutely critical in my making decisions that would ultimately impact my future. Mentors are critical in forming a young adult dream.

Sustaining Images

The wonderful book *Common Fire: Leading Lives of Commitment in a Complex World*[10] is a study by a group of scholars who interviewed numerous people in their thirties and forties who were still making a difference in the world for what they called the "common good" of humanity. The focus of the book was not students who showed commitment and faith during their college years but those who held on to their convictions *after the college years*. When those people were asked what sustained them throughout their twenties and into their forties—despite difficult and taxing experiences—one of the consistent answers revolved around having *a dream*.

Rather than speaking of dreams, the authors discussed the importance of people having "sustaining images" to guide their decision making. "Sustaining images" are mental pictures that motivate people to maintain their commitments—year after year. To the researchers' surprise, these images were not always dreams of justice or visions of a perfect world. Rather, the sustaining images were glimpses of injustices, cruelty, and suffering that they had witnessed in their childhood or college years. It was these indelible images, etched in their minds and hearts, that gave them the motivation to keep at their work. Those images showed what could be or what needed to change in the world. One white man remembered as a teenager seeing a play called *In White America*, which exposed him to white oppression. Those impressions led to his involvement in racial reconciliation. Another woman, who now works on behalf of families and children, recalled the rape scene in the film "Two Women" and remembered leaving the film totally overwhelmed by the vulnerability of women. Those images have stayed with those people and others and have fueled their commitments.

A friend of mine, Sean Closky, headed up a Catholic-based housing program in Camden, New Jersey. St. Joseph's Carpenter

Society is an amazing organization that is slowly changing the look of our community. Sean and his colleagues are building affordable housing and giving poor people a chance to buy these homes that were once scarred, abandoned buildings or vacant lots. What sustains Sean as he attacks this huge and daunting project of trying to make a community more livable? He has an image of what neighborhoods *should* look like and how people *should* view their neighborhoods. Sean's dream is to create a hometown that is safe, has nice parks, and does not harbor abandoned buildings and crack houses. His dream is that children can play in the streets and residents can take the iron bars off their windows. Streets can be paved and bordered with trees and plants. That's Sean's *sustaining image*. He believes that God wants all people—not just the wealthy—to live in neighborhoods that foster life and hope. Sean patiently puts up with all the city politics, the red tape, the funding problems, and the legal issues, because he has a sustaining image, a dream.

Finding a Dream: Sustaining Images

Sometimes God puts things in our minds because those ideas are supposed to guide us and give us courage for the future. Those images are communicated through different forms—literature, the arts, movies, experiences, and a host of other media. With the help of God's Spirit, those images can plant themselves in our minds and hearts and provide clarity.

Statistics have always provided a kind of image for me. When I see statistics that highlight gross injustices in our world, something ignites deep within me. Sure, statistics can often be manipulated or presented in ways that do not project the whole truth, but there is something about viewing comparative data that just hits me. Consider the following statistics cited in a 1995 study by Bryant Myers called "The State of the World's Children"[11]:

1. In third-world countries more than 100 million children are growing up on the streets. Six hundred million people live in slums today. Of those millions, 74 percent are under the age of twenty-four. Many of these children grow up with no education, little affection, and no adult guidance. What happens to these children? In some cities they are hunted and shot like stray dogs and cats.

2. Almost one million of the children are forced into prostitution. In the city of Bombay almost one-third of the prostitutes are little girls. In Bangkok 800,000 girls under the age of sixteen are forced into prostitution. Those little ones are subjected to horrendous abuse, infectious diseases, and treatment that most of us cannot even imagine.

3. No third-world city has a *median* age greater than 20. Thus cities are filled with youth. The United States has only 28 million teens, only 3 percent of the world's youth. Ironically, 99 percent of the world's youth workers minister to less than 3 percent of the world's teens, since the United States has 99 percent of the world's youth workers.

4. One-half of the world's 36 million refugees are displaced children who will grow up without a home, often living in refugee camps.

5. In some villages in Africa, 100 percent of the population is HIV-positive. In other parts of Africa, more than 50 percent of the population is infected with HIV. Many parents will die and orphan their children.

6. Closer to home, in our cities 3,000 children and teens will drop out of school every day. Before the end of the school year, 600,000 children and teens will be lost. In some of America's urban settings nearly 50 percent of the youth will drop out of school before their twelfth grade. More than 130,000 kids nationally will take guns to school each day.

7. Between 1985 and 1991 the number of young men between ages 16 and 22 who were killed in the United States increased 154 percent. Since 1960 the rate at which teens took their lives has tripled. Each year the justice system spends $20 billion to arrest, rehabilitate, and jail juvenile offenders—only to watch 70 percent of those incarcerated and released commit crimes again.

8. Although a slight decline in recent years, the number of teen girls having babies has increased 200 percent in the last 30 years.

I could go on and on with more statistics that reveal gross injustices and extensive social problems within our world. As Christians, who believe that all people are made in the image of God, we should be bothered when we read such horrendous statistics. We should be bothered when we cannot find the presence of the church—the body of Christ—in our communities and areas of greatest need. For some of you, statistics should get under your skin and cause you to ask the questions: What can I *do*? How can my life make a difference? How can my skills, talents, and education be used to better the conditions of God's children who suffer so deeply? Allow God's Spirit to put a dream in your heart and mind—a dream of a better world.

If Jesus Were a Senior

The world offers many kinds of dreams. There are the dreams of financial success and security—the big house, a nice car, and regular vacations with all of life's amenities. There also is the dream of power and recognition—to be successful, to be noticed, to be an important person. There is the dream of the *perfect* job, or the *perfect* partner or the *perfect* life—whatever that may look like. The media insistently bombard us with their different kinds of dreams. Many of those dreams are antithetical to the biblical witness, contradicting the intentions of God.

One of the most vivid contradictions of dreams in the Scripture is the conflict between Peter and Jesus. Peter has his dream of what Jesus' life should be about and the kind of leader Jesus should be. I can only imagine that Peter had visions of one day playing an important role in Jesus' kingdom—a kingdom where Jesus would liberate his country from Roman occupation and rule from a position of power. Peter would have all the perks of being in Jesus' cabinet. Maybe he would even get a street named after him. But then Jesus began to explain to his disciples that he must suffer and ultimately be killed. Whoa, wait a minute, that's not the way it should go! So Peter stepped in to rebuke Jesus. "God forbid it, Lord! This must never happen to you" (Matt. 16:22). Jesus' response was one of the most dramatic in Scripture. Matthew records that "he turned and said to Peter, 'Get behind me, Satan! You are a stumbling block to me; for you are setting your mind not on divine things but on human things.'" The two dreams of the future clashed. Peter dreamed of a kingdom modeled on worldly paradigms; Jesus dreamed of a kingdom that would be birthed when people surrendered their wills to the intentions of God. Jesus further spelled out his vision of his kingdom when he claimed, "If any want to become my followers, let them deny themselves and take up their cross and follow me" (Matt. 16:24). Even though

Peter probably had the best intentions, his dream for Jesus' life was still misguided.

Jesus had a dream. His dream was for God's kingdom to find expression in the world—through people and structures. The term *God's kingdom* is best described by the Hebrew word *shalom*—a community of peace, wholeness, and prosperity for *all* those who dwell together. Jesus wanted a world where love existed among all people, where there were no poor people, where the sick could be healed, and where all people could live in communion with God and not be excluded from worship because of race or social status. As Jesus healed, fed, and demonstrated love to those he touched, he was giving witness to his dream. It was that dream that guided Jesus in his earthly ministry.

"Where there is no vision, the people perish," claims the author of Proverbs (29:18 KJV). Likewise, where there is no dream, the disciple of Jesus slowly perishes. So cultivate a dream for your life—not a self-centered, self-serving kind of dream, but a God dream. It must be a dream that is given by God, one that will generously and joyfully benefit other people and expand God's witness in the world. When this kind of dream is imparted to you, then you can embrace the words of the Scottish writer George MacDonald, who said, "When a man [or woman] dreams his own dream, he is the sport of his dream; when Another gives it him, that Other is able to fulfill it." When God gives us a dream, God also provides the resources needed to fulfill the dream.

A Conversation with Jesus

My former roommate Bob has a dream of traveling around the world one day—skiing in the Alps, sailing in the South Pacific, drinking coffee at sidewalk cafés in Paris. Jack, down the hall, dreams of one day owning a summer home on a lake; he wants a speedboat. Kent dreams of having a million dollars by the age of 30—hoping to have started and sold his first company. Sarah dreams of becoming the first lawyer in her family, maybe even taking a case to the Supreme Court.

"Their dreams are too small!" came the Voice from the top bunk. "I know what you're thinking."

How did my Friend know what I was thinking? Perhaps my thoughts are confused with my prayers. Whatever the case, I was busted.

"I wasn't praying, you know?" I protested. "Is there no privacy in this relationship?"

"It's all the same to me," continued the familiar Voice.

"What do you mean, their dreams are too small?" I questioned. "They sound pretty good to me."

"Anybody can do those things. God wants to give you a dream that is beyond your reach. You know, the kind of dream that is overwhelming. The kind of dream that can be fulfilled only with God's help."

I had to chuckle. Why would I want a dream that is "overwhelming" and "beyond" my reach? This was not conventional wisdom. So I asked the question.

"Why would I want a dream that is overwhelming?" I was trying to make sense out of this illogical proposition.

There was silence. I waited.

"Let me put it this way," began my Friend. "A person grows in faith when they are put in situations that call them beyond their own abilities. Quite frankly, the world is a mess and needs a few more faith-filled people who will embrace some outrageous dreams."

"What would an outrageous dream look like?" I asked with a high degree of curiosity.

I braced myself for the reply. "How about building schools for kids in places where there are no schools? How about digging wells in communities were there are no wells for water? How about opening health clinics in communities where there are no health clinics, or creating orphanages for street children who have no place to live, or helping to relieve third-world debt, or to reform prison systems, or . . ."

At this point I had to cut my Friend off. The ideas were flowing. "OK, OK, I think I understand," I interrupted.

"You need a worthy dream." I listened with intent. The words were beginning to make sense. "You need a dream that will help you live your life with a sense of urgency and purpose—a dream that will lift you above the trivial distractions of life. You need to pray that God will give you a vision for a task too big for your own doing."

And then I was left alone to ponder the words. My room was dark and silent.

Remember:

All men [or women] dream; but not equally.
Those who dream by night in the dusty
Recesses of their minds
Awake to find that it was vanity;
But the dreamers of day arc dangerous men,
That they may act their dreams with open
eyes to make it possible.

T. E. Lawrence, *The Seven Pillars of Wisdom*

Reflections for Students

1. What is the difference between a "God-given" dream and a personal dream? Can they be the same?

2. Do you have a God-given dream for your life? If so, share it with the group? If not, how do you think God might share a dream with you?

3. Who is a "dreamer" you admire? How does the dream motivate that person? How does the dream sustain that person?

4. What preparations can you make to open yourself to the dreams of God for your life?

For the Leader

Find some examples within the annals of church history of people who dared to dream. Share with your students how those individuals acquired those dreams, how those dreams influenced their decision making, and how those dreams sustained them during difficult times. Have your students outline some ways they might be able to begin opening themselves to the dreams of God for their lives.

Meditation

Lord,

Grant me the courage to ask for a dream—a vision for my life.
Help me to let go of the agendas and ambitions that might close my mind and heart to your dreams.
Take away those aspects of my life that blind me and numb me to your Spirit.

You give dreams in different ways.
Open my heart,
    my mind,
    my consciousness
    to your creative ways of communication.

And Lord,
When you give me a dream that is beyond my abilities,
Remind me that you are the author and ultimately will fulfill
    the dream.

Amen

Chapter 2

Travel Preparations:
It's Not the Road You Travel

The kind of peace that the world gives
is the peace we experience when for a little time the world
    happens to be peaceful.
It is a peace that lasts for only as long as the peaceful
    time lasts
because as soon as the peaceful time ends, the peace
    ends with it.
The peace Jesus offers, on the other hand,
has nothing to do with the things that are going on at the
    moment
he offers it, which are for the most part tragic and terrible
    things.
It is a profound and inward peace that sees with unflinching
    clarity
the tragic and terrible things that are happening
and yet is not shattered by them. . . .
His peace comes not from the world
but from something whole and holy within himself
which sees the world also as whole and holy
because deep beneath all the broken and unholy things that
    are happening
in it even as he speaks, Jesus sees what he calls the
    Kingdom of God.

                  Frederick Buechner, *Longing for Home*

A New Twist on an Old Parable

I just have to tell you, Vern, those words you shared a few weeks ago have stayed with me," said George, sitting to my right. The staff and I were sitting on folding chairs in a circle saying good-bye to Vern. George took a breath and then continued.

"When I asked if you would go through the experience of being unemployed for the last two years again, you surprised me. That was strange but powerful when you said *yes*."

29

Vern nodded and smiled from across the room in his quiet, humble way. As a talented and brilliant cancer research scientist with a Ph.D., he had been without a job for two years. His previous biotech company had been mismanaged, and he had been laid off. As a man in his early fifties who had been used to living on a six-figure income, he discovered that finding a company to employ him was a difficult task—regardless of his qualifications. For two years this gifted scientist had interviewed around the world—Canada, Switzerland, Denmark, and across the United States. Time after time he had been rejected. "You're too qualified." "When we get our financing together, we'll bring you on." "You're one of our first choices." Too often he didn't even get the courtesy of a return call.

However, in between interviews, Vern did our youth program's janitorial work, volunteered at his church, and endured the repeated humiliation of friends asking if he had found work. I felt guilty watching this world-class scientist—a number of patents to his claim—clean the toilets at our ministry and set up chairs. But he did everything without complaining; he worked humbly. He became an example of servanthood to many. Some even called him Saint Vern.

"What God has done in my life could not have happened if I had not been laid off," he began softly. "It sounds strange, but I'm thankful for this *season of winter*."

Vern was sincere. It was not just false humility shared in an attempt to downplay the fact that he had just been offered a fantastic new job—the reason we were all in the room celebrating. He really meant it. Vern really believed that the rejection, the humiliation, the depression, and the feelings of futility of the last twenty-four months had all been important to his growth. He would not have changed a thing—we all believed it, and his sincerity spoke volumes to those in the room.

Then Vern began to muse about some of life's lessons. "You know, I've read a lot of Søren Kierkegaard in the last few months."

Immediately my ears perked up. Kierkegaard is one of my favorite philosophers and Christian theologians, a Danish thinker who had an incredibly creative and perceptive mind. He was also an outspoken critic of the church in the nineteenth century. I was intrigued that Vern had discovered the writings of this man, for Kierkegaard was not someone currently found on the Christian bestseller list. It takes work to find his books; it takes work to understand them.

Vern continued, "In a reflection Kierkegaard wrote about the story of the Good Samaritan, he claimed that the important part of life was not the road we travel, it is how we traveled the road. He reminded us that Jesus' parable had three people going down the same road; only one stopped to do what was right and good. All three travelers were on the same road. *But the road didn't matter*. What mattered was how they traveled the road."

By this point Vern was sounding more like a philosopher than a research specialist. His thoughts came out of the many hours he had to read and reflect—time that he never would have had if he had not lost his job. During those dark and lonely hours, when he wondered how he was going to make the next mortgage payment and support his family, Vern was really able to take stock of his life. He thought more deeply about *how he was traveling his road*. His dark night of the soul gave him a new perspective from which he had gleaned very valuable insights. Whether he was scrubbing toilets or finding a cure for cancer was irrelevant. Whether employed or volunteering, it was the same. What really mattered to him was how he had been traveling his road.

So often in life we never get the opportunity to get off *our* road long enough to examine how we are traveling. Rather, we become so focused on our road that we critically fail to examine *how* we are traveling that road. Like hamsters on an exercise wheel, we become so busy that we never pause long enough to gain perspective on where we are going or whether we are traveling the road well.

What Kierkegaard insightfully wrote about the parable is that Jesus affirms the man who stopped and cared for others. The Samaritan was a man who traveled his road of life *well*. Who he was, what he did for a living, and where he was going were inconsequential.

The great thing about our Christian experience is that we can invite God into the most difficult of our life situations and end up saying, "I wouldn't change a thing." We can acknowledge with Paul that "all things work together for good for those who love God" (Rom. 8:28). And then, like my friend Vern, we pass those life lessons on to others that will hear—even the difficult and painful lessons.

Life Is Difficult

M. Scott Peck's best-selling book of a few years ago, *The Road Less Traveled*, begins with a classic line: "Life is difficult." Peck tells his readers that life is not always fair, not always fun, and definitely not always easy. Embrace the fact, claims Peck, that there will not always be a green pasture. Rather than trying to avoid the hardships of life, Peck challenges his readers to embrace them, grow from them, and become stronger through them. The road of life creates bumps and bruises, and it is best that one quickly learn how to deal with difficulties.

However, in the United States many are currently enjoying a high standard of living because of revolutionary medical breakthroughs, a robust economy, and opportunities for education. The World Trade Center and Pentagon terrorist attacks in 2001 notwithstanding, Americans have lived relatively protected lives and enjoyed the fruits of freedom and wealth. We expect a good life. Living in a society that for many years had not experienced the trauma of war, famine, or widespread disease, many feel it is their divine right not to suffer.

Consequently, many Christians spend their lives trying to find *the perfect road* to travel. Rather than embracing the road that they are on—and learning to travel that road well—they don't live life in the moment. If they have a job, they still entertain the idea of a better one. If they live in a small house, they dream of yet a bigger one. If they scrape by financially each month, they fantasize about having more money. If they have annoying friends or family members, they dream of the day they will have *real* friends. If they find that their church is not perfect, they quickly move to the next. Too frequently people in our culture spend all their time trying to find utopia.

Advertisers and the media have capitalized on this angst. They try to convince us that what we have is not enough—that the life we lead is not complete without their product. With more—a better car, a remodeled kitchen, a better body, a better computer—we can get off the mundane, uneventful road we are presently traveling and have something better! Of course, we all know the end result. We quickly become bored with the latest gimmick and begin to look for another.

The problem is that this mind-set has trickled into the subconscious of the Christian church as well. Many feel that a strong faith or a blessed life means an *easy life*. Many associate God's presence in their lives with a divine right to comfort, abundant provision, and success. Christians have been brainwashed to believe that if one is really in the will of God, then their life will be one euphoric moment after another—rather like a day at Disney World with an endless supply of cotton candy.

The downside of this skewed view of life is that when one encounters tough times, he or she begins to question faith and God. Far too often I have heard statements like "If only I were living more faithfully, this never would have happened" or "Why isn't God blessing me, I'm doing all the right things." Rather than trying to discover what God is doing through the difficulty, embracing the challenges, and growing because of them, we complain and try to fill our disappointments with stuff. But Scriptures and church history suggest something quite different from what our culturally sanitized faith suggests. The truth is that the more faithfully and prophetically one decides to live, the more *difficult* and *painful* one's road can be. Therefore, one of the challenges for a Christian is to develop a mind-set that counters the messages of our culture.

Developing a Biblical Habit of Mind

Happily, the Bible offers us an alternative message to those of our culture. When we allow ourselves to develop a mind-set that is rooted in the biblical message, we develop a habit that allows us to filter out the pervasive messages of our culture. Or at least we begin to look at our culture with a degree of objectivity—thus embracing a lifestyle that is not rooted in fantasies.

The apostle Paul developed a mind-set that didn't allow him to run from the road he was traveling but, rather, helped him to travel more passionately and faithfully the road he was on. We never read about Paul after his blinding conversion trying to escape God's call. Rather, we encounter him living faithfully in the midst of adversity.

The book of 2 Corinthians communicates Paul's mind-set in a powerful manner. He is able to look at any circumstance and redeem it into something wonderful. Eugene Peterson's *The Message* translates Paul's thoughts, dramatically contrasting his circumstances with his attitudinal response. Look for these contrasts as you read this passage.

> We've been surrounded and battered by troubles, but we're not demoralized; we're not sure what we do, but we know that God knows what to do; we've been spiritually terrorized, but God hasn't left our side; we've been thrown down, but we haven't been broken. . . . Our lives are at constant risk for Jesus' sake, which makes Jesus' life all the more evident in us. While we're going through the worst, you're getting in on the best. . . .

> Even though on the outside it often looks like things
> are falling apart on us, on the inside, where God is mak-
> ing new life, not a day goes by without his unfolding grace.
> These hard times are small potatoes compared to the
> coming good times. . . .
>   Cramped conditions here don't get us down. They
> only remind us of the spacious living conditions ahead.
> . . . Rumored to be dead; beaten within an inch of our
> lives, but refusing to die; immersed in tears, yet always
> filled with deep joy; living on handouts, yet enriching
> many; having nothing, having it all.
>   2 Cor. 4:8–12; 4:16–17; 5:6; 6:8–10, THE MESSAGE

This translation underscores Paul's incredible ability to turn
dismal situations into opportunities to meet God in new ways.
Paul finds God's presence in the middle of difficulties. He does
not whine because God is not blessing his life with material
comforts. Rather, he is rooted in the belief that "all things work
for the good of those who love God." Thus he lives with a sense
of peace and assurance—even when his world seems to be falling
apart.

What intrigues me about Paul is that he did more than just
memorize his Old Testament Scriptures. Rather, he internalized
the promises of God and walked his life road fully convinced
that God could and would redeem any situation—in spite of difficult and trying external circumstances. Paul had come to a
place in his life in which circumstances did not really matter. He
breathed hope. He developed an intimacy with God that
allowed him to be confident that every situation provided
opportunity. For me, Paul embodies a faith perspective that we
should all try to embody when it comes to trials. Just imagine:
we *can* reach a point in our lives when circumstances do not dictate our attitudes and destiny!

I have frequently heard the phrase "So and so is such a
mature Christian" or "So and so is a person of great faith."
When I hear those comments, they usually are about dynamic
preachers who articulate deep biblical principles or those who
have memorized vast amounts of Scripture. Certainly they are
great attributes to possess, but they are not what truly define the
mature Christian. The mature Christian is someone who, in the
midst of adversity or grave injustice, can find joy and maintain
an intimacy with God. While traveling a difficult road, people
with mature faith find meaning and grow from the experience.
Authentic faith does not magically lift the believer off the road;

rather, authentic faith enables the person to engage difficulty while producing the fruits of a Spirit-filled life.

Karl Marx coined the phrase "Religion is the opiate of the people," for he saw religious people using their faith to escape responsibilities and difficulties. Our faith should never be used as a mechanism to escape reality. Our faith should help us redeem our existing reality and make something good out of this reality.

Do I Need to Pretend That Everything Is Fine?

Are anger, doubt, fear, sadness, and despair legitimate feelings? Does one have to pretend these feelings do not exist and put on a mask of perfection? As Christians, are we required to put on a happy face and deny the realities of what is going on around us? Simply, no.

Rather, feelings are legitimate and need to be expressed. But there is a difference between expressing our feelings and allowing our feelings to control our lives and ultimately control our destiny and faith. Jesus is probably the prime example of what it means for a person to express feelings and yet stay on the road. The money changers desecrating the temple enraged him, and he responded appropriately. Then in the Garden of Gethsemane Jesus knew that he would die a vicious, ugly, painful death. On his knees he begged God to prevent the suffering. The text records that Jesus was sorrowful—*to the point of death*. Yes, he expressed feelings. And yet, in the garden, Jesus embraced the greater will of God. Jesus expressed feelings but did not attempt to escape his situation. His prayers and struggles called him to embrace his future, not escape to something easier.

How Do We Travel the Road?

Amazing things can happen when we develop the discipline of asking God to travel with us. When we invite God into our circumstances, we find ourselves living life more intensely—much more full of God. We also discover one of the important truths of life: *there are no ordinary circumstances*. For the ordinary comes alive with God's Spirit when God is invited to direct and participate.

A few years ago one of my staff shared a story that vividly illustrates this principle of inviting God into our circumstances. It is a simple story, but it captures a philosophy of life:

Our broken and bruised school bus sputtered on its way home on the Atlantic City Expressway. None of the motorists speeding in the other direction toward the casinos realized that something sacred was taking place on the inside of our aging white bus. Our windows were fogged, the heater was on the blink, and the back window had been shattered by a vandal's beer bottle. Yet our bus limped along like a proud relic across from luxury buses, equipped with television sets and bars, that raced past in the opposite direction to deposit eager gamblers in Atlantic City. But our wounded bus was filled with the voices of sixty-five first- and second-graders, singing full-throated Christmas carols—*Silent Night, Joy to the World, Go Tell It on the Mountain*—that caressed the afternoon air and floated heavenward.

Was our dilapidated bus a church on the expressway? Sure. Our packed, aging, unassuming bus had become a glowing sanctuary.

"Pure joy," exalted Gina, our children's director, as she relayed the story when she returned back home. "It sent shivers up and down my spine. The Spirit was with us," she radiated.

The children had had a lot to be joyful about. They were returning from UrbanPromise's Annual First- and Second-Grade Retreat—an action-packed twenty-four hours of swimming, staying up late, and eating loads of McDonald's food. Our experienced, talented, deeply committed staff created a high-energy, non-stop action program that also gave them time to build trust, model God's love, and share the Christmas story.

But it wasn't until the bus ride home that God really moved.

Bus rides with kids can be boring, wasted time, a necessity, a headache, and a means to an end. But when God's Spirit is invited into a bus ride, the time is redeemed and marvelous things happen. An old, rickety bus becomes a cathedral.

That afternoon two different kinds of people were traveling the same road. Both were in buses. Both traveled the same distance. The major difference was *how the people traveled the road*. One group tried to escape the futility of their existence by numbing their minds with small-screened televisions and dry martinis. The other group had a sacred experience, met God in a special way, and transformed a normally mundane trip into a journey they would never forget. What mattered was not the road they traveled, but how they traveled the road.

Since then, my staff has become terrific at redeeming bus and van rides. Frequently they share that the best discussions they have with children and teens with whom they work are on the van rides after programs. Rather than dreading the tough city driving, the screaming kids, or the belligerent teens, they turn these moments into lively discussions. They invite God onto the road. It may sound simplistic, but their attitude makes all the difference. Their attitude makes challenging and difficult ministry even easier to endure and persevere.

The Dancing Toll Taker

Dr. Charles Garfield tells a wonderful story about an interesting character he met one day while traveling over the San Francisco-Oakland Bay Bridge. He had traveled the bridge thousands of times, yet never had an exchange with a toll taker that was worth remembering . . . until one morning in 1984.

Dr. Garfield was headed for lunch in San Francisco as he drove toward one of the tollbooths. He heard loud rock music. It was so loud that it penetrated his closed window and drowned out the talk radio show he was listening to. The music blared like a wild party or rock concert. Garfield looked around. There were no other cars with their windows open, no sound was coming from any of the trucks. He looked at the tollbooth. Inside was a man *dancing!*

Pulling up to pay his toll, Garfield asked, "What are you doing?"

"I'm having a party," said the toll taker.

"All by yourself? What about the other toll takers?" Garfield looked over at the other booths; nothing was moving.

"They're not invited."

Garfield had a dozen other questions for the dancing man, but the person behind him started beeping his horn. Garfield drove off but made a note that he needed to find that guy again. There was something in his eye that said there was magic in that tollbooth.

Months later he did find him again, still with loud music, still having a party. Again he asked, "What are you doing?"

He said, "I remember you from the last time. I'm still dancing. I'm having the same party."

Garfield said, "Look, what about the rest of those toll takers?"

He said, "Stop. What do those booths look like to you?" He pointed down the row of tollbooths.

"They look like tollbooths," replied Garfield

"Nooooo, imagination! Use your imagination!" urged the toll taker.

In exasperation Garfield yielded, "OK, I give up. What do they look like to *you*?"

"Vertical coffins!"

"What are you talking about?" questioned Garfield.

"Well, at 8:30 every morning, live people get in to their booths, then they die. At 4:30, like Lazarus from the dead, they emerge and go home. For eight hours their brains are on hold, dead on the job, going through the motions."

Garfield was amazed. This guy had developed a philosophy, a mythology about his job. He could not help asking the next question: "Why is it different for you? You seem to be having a good time."

"I knew you were going to ask that," said the toll taker. "I'm going to be a dancer someday." He pointed to the administration building. "My bosses are in there, and they're paying for my training."

According to the dancing toll taker, sixteen people were dead on the job, but the seventeenth, in precisely the same situation, figured out a way to live. That man was having a party on his job where you and I would not last three days. The boredom!

Several days later Garfield and the toll taker had lunch. The toll taker, now known as Sam, said, "I don't understand why anybody would think my job is boring. I have a corner office, glass on all sides, I can see the Golden Gate Bridge, San Francisco, the Berkeley Hills every day; half the Western world vacations here, and I just stroll in every day and practice dancing."

How can one develop a mind-set like the "dancing tollbooth worker?"

Most of us, if we are honest, probably would be like the majority of the tollbooth workers—we would endure the day, go through the numbing motions, and dream about what we are going to do after we get off work. But we *could*, like Sam, choose to use our circumstances creatively and joyously. We could ask God's Spirit to breath life into our reality and transform our less-than-ideal circumstance into an experience that moves us closer toward the likeness of Christ. There may be times in our lives when we have no control over our circumstances. We do have control as to whether we invite God into those circumstances.

If Jesus Were a Senior

The later years of college can be filled with optimism and anticipation for the future. They can also be filled with fear, a sense of dislocation, or agonizing moments when critical decisions need to be made. One's future can seem very uncertain. But in the midst of this uncertainty, one thing can be guaranteed: events and situations will not always go our way. Some people will get caught in seemingly dead-end jobs. Others will encounter unfair breaks and lose everything. Some will suffer from health problems. We cannot know ahead of time the circumstances of the road we will end up traveling. What we can know, however, is that we will travel a road. The question is, What will be the depth of our faith? Will circumstances dictate how we live our lives? Or will our hope in God's ability to redeem difficult circumstances be so rooted in our lives that our circumstances will have little control over how we live?

One of the most remarkable aspects of Jesus' message was its constant challenge for us to engage in *this* life. Jesus seldom talked about heaven. Jesus never taught a doctrine that calls his followers to disengage from daily responsibility and head for the mountaintop to live in isolation. Jesus' teaching is about the here and now. The faith he calls his followers to live out is no crutch for those looking for an easier road. His Sermon on the Mount (Matthew 5–7) is probably the most poignant example. He said astoundingly:

> Love your enemies.
> Be peacemakers.
> Do not lust.
> Turn the other cheek.
> Give to the needy.
> Pray in your closet.
> Don't be hypocritical about your faith.

Jesus' teachings call one to *wrestle* with the difficulties of life and *infuse* those challenges with a different attitude and perspective. As a matter of fact, when our circumstances take a turn for the worse—"when people revile you and persecute you and utter all kinds of evil against you falsely on my account. Rejoice and be glad," Jesus taught. Thus, his teachings call the believer to a life of challenge and full engagement in the world—regardless of the circumstances.

Jesus Wants to Talk

"I'm tired of your complaining," came the Voice beside me. I had not seen anyone when I first entered the empty chapel. I wanted to get away. I wanted to escape. The last thing I wanted was to talk.

"I know what you are thinking," continued the Intruder. "You've come here to pray and get away from it all. Well, guess what, you're not the only one who gets to talk. If you're going to pray, you better get ready to listen, too."

I did not like the attitude of my intrusive Friend—always showing up at inopportune moments and places. A chapel, of all places! I'd had a rough day. My job had dragged on forever. All sorts of people wanted my help. (I work at the library in the periodicals section. When I'm there, I usually get to catch up on a little sleep.) My car wouldn't start, so I couldn't meet my friends for dinner and had to eat in the cafeteria with a bunch of freshmen.

"Why don't you just leave me alone," I whispered.

"Because I need you to learn a few lessons. You're going to be heading out into the real world soon, and I'm afraid that you're not going to make it."

"What do you mean, 'I'm not going to make it'?"

"You don't respond too well to adversity," continued the Voice. "You let your circumstances dictate the way you express your faith. You need to begin to see opportunity in adversity. Today was nothing compared to what you're going to experience after you graduate."

My Companion paused for a minute, but I knew the lecture was just beginning. "You could have really helped people in the library this afternoon. Remember that guy who needed the article on medieval literature? He was really stressed. You could have helped him. But you were in such a rush you didn't notice how panicked he looked."

I thought for a moment. Yes, I did remember that kid. A word of encouragement or a little extra help probably would have eased his stress.

"And dinner. Those freshmen who were eating at your table? They need an older role model. But you were too busy sulking about your car.

They needed a senior to take the time to listen and ask them about their experience."

OK, so I knew the words were true. I was letting my circumstances dictate my reactions; I was not traveling my road very well. My self-centeredness was blinding me from seeing the needs of others.

"Learn to travel well, now," added my friend, "because it will only get harder."

And then I was alone, left to myself to think.

Recently a very good friend of mine died from cancer at the age of fifty-five. Helen battled the disease for over ten years. She did everything medically possible to try and fight the illness, but in the end the cancer came back and destroyed her body. If anyone should have been bitter and angry, it was Helen. Her cancer was misdiagnosed and went undetected for close to two years. If the doctor had caught it initially, Helen could have been restored to full health.

Every time I went to visit Helen, I was overcome with a sense of peace and love. Up until the end, she maintained her sense of humor and was an incredible testimony to God's presence in the midst of difficult circumstances. As a matter of fact, the last time I visited her—a few days before she died—we laughed so hard that the hospice worker had to tell us to stop. The worker was afraid Helen would die laughing. Toward the end, Helen was no more than a frail skeleton of a human body. But she never stopped smiling. And as long as I have lived, I have never met anybody who has traveled her road so well. For Helen, traveling well did not mean curling up in a ball and giving up. Helen looked her disease in the face and fought it with every ounce of energy she possessed. But she also invited God into her difficult circumstances and evidenced God's presence in all aspects of her suffering. Because of this attitude, Helen reflected God's heart in the midst of trying circumstances. The lives of many people were changed because of her testimony.

Few of us really know what road we will end up traveling. The road will change. Jobs will come and go. Unexpected health issues will surface. Relationships will take unexpected turns. There is a good chance we will end up heading in a life direction that we never imagined. Regardless, the actual road we walk is not so important; rather, it is the compassion, the grace, the joy, and the generosity we display along the way.

Remember:

The longer I live, the more I realize the impact of attitude on life. Attitude, to me, is more important than education, than money, than circumstances, than failures, than success, than what other people think or say or do. It is more important than appearance, giftedness, or skill. It will make or break a company . . . a church . . . a home. We have a choice every day regarding the attitude we embrace for that day. We cannot change our past . . . we cannot change the fact that people act in a certain way. We cannot change the inevitable. The only thing we can do is play on the one string we have, and that is our attitude . . . I am convinced that life is 10% what happens to me and 90% how I react to it. And so it is with you . . . we are in charge of our attitudes.

Charles Swindol, "Attitudes"

Reflections for Students

1. How do difficult life circumstances impact your faith and feeling about God?

2. How will you move to a place in your life where your faith will be less determined by external circumstances?

3. Do you believe that a life of faithfulness to God should guarantee blessing? If so, why?

4. Identify a mundane or difficult circumstance in your life today. How might you invite God into that circumstance so that you can demonstrate God's love and grow through the situation?

For the Leader

Ask the students to share a specific example of someone who traveled the road well. What difficulty did that person encounter? How did that person respond to the difficulty that confronted him or her on the road? How did he or she grow through the experience?

Meditation

Lord,

I do not know what my life road will entail.
I do not know the turns it will take, the bumps, or the obstacles.
I do not know whom I will meet.
But I do know that I will travel.

Help me to walk the road well.
Protect me from becoming like those who turned their eye from
   need, whose hearts were not filled with compassion,
   who did not walk in a way that reflected your heart and
   courage.

And when difficulties come my way,
Remind me to invite you to redeem the troubles,
Remind me to learn from every experience and every encounter,
Remind me not to seek the escapes of this world.

Teach me to transform toll booths into dance studios,
Broken-down buses into cathedrals of praise,
And inconvenience into opportunity to share your love.

Amen

Chapter 3

Calling Preparations:
Discovering Our Uniqueness

*A sense of calling
should precede a choice of job and career,
and the main way to discover a calling is along the line of
what we are each created and gifted to be.
Instead of, "You are what you do,"
calling says: "Do what you are."*

Os Guinness, The Call

*Then the first question to ask is not, "what do I want to do with
my life?" It is not as if I first come to know myself and then choose
a vocation that fulfills and satisfies me. For it is only by hearing
and answering the divine summons, by participating in my calling, that I can come to know who I am. We are not who we think
we are; we are who God calls us to be.*

Gilbert Meilaender

Stumbling into My Calling

I rushed through my rounds and went through my mental checklist: lock the windows, shut off the lights, and bolt the auxiliary doors. It had been another long day. I glanced at my watch—11:30 P.M.! All I could think of was laying my head on my pillow and catching a few hours. Tomorrow the activity would start again—another day of directing a summer day camp for 150 energetic inner-city kids. And I was still just a college student.

I stepped out onto the cement stoop in the balmy July night and tripped over something soft. I retracted my step and flipped the light switch. There, cuddled like a kitten, lay the body of a little boy, sound asleep. It was Peanut!

Peanut was a neighborhood kid who had been attending our day camp for the past few days. I scooped him up and loaded him in our van. All I could think of was getting him home. His mother had to be worried sick—her five-year-old baby wandering dangerous streets in the middle of the night!

At a little past midnight I stood outside his apartment door in one of the tougher housing projects in the city. I cradled my sleepy friend against my shoulder and waited for someone to answer the door. I could hear the television blaring inside, but nobody seemed to notice. I banged the door with my fist, hoping not to wake up the neighbors. The door slowly opened. It was Peanut's four-year-old sister.

Surprised to see a four-year-old still awake after midnight, I asked, "Is your mom home?"

"No."

"Your grandma?" She just shook her head.

I peered into the apartment. No furniture. No pictures on the wall. Just a little black-and-white television with a coat-hanger antenna and a few Chinese food containers and potato-chip bags littering the corner of the room.

Peanut's brother, who didn't bother to look up, was lying on the stained carpet, his eyes glued to the fuzzy images on the television. He was seven.

"When is your mom going to be home?" I asked. The kids didn't answer. Their lack of concern for their mother's whereabouts shocked me. My mind couldn't embrace what I was witnessing. Three children under the age of seven, home alone with no babysitter, no phone, no beds, and no food.

And there I was, a college junior, raised in the comforts of a protective, upper-middle-class, suburban, two-parent family. The scene I stepped into never would have happened in my home. It never would have happened in the neighborhood in which I was raised—a mother leaving little ones to fend for themselves. I could not conceive of a five-year-old boy wandering the streets at midnight, not being missed by anybody.

My life would never be the same.

I was at a crossroad. Family and friends were beginning to ask the big question, "What are you going to do with your life?" I didn't know!

After high school I had spent a year as a stock trader on the floor of a small exchange in the Pacific Northwest. At night, I studied for a brokerage license, an exciting time. Young men and women who worked with me spent their days flipping stocks and making thousands of dollars. It was an easy way to make a fast dollar. Those same people were now driving to work in their Porsches and BMWs. Surely I could upgrade my '76 VW Bug if I could get in on the action. The hours were great, leaving all kinds of time for leisure. This could make a pretty good life.

Then the stock market took one of its famous plunges, and I realized the fragility of that kind of life.

College began to sound like a good idea, and I began to save. But then I got a hot tip and invested my tuition money in a small mining company that was about to release its latest exploration reports. Since the market had already slumped, and since the soil samples were "rich in valuable minerals," I was assured that my investment would yield enough to cover a few years of college. I bit the hook. Two weeks later my stock crashed. The company was investigated and eventually collapsed. My tuition was gone.

I ended up earning tuition by spending the summer on a garbage truck, slinging trash. Every hot, steamy, smelly fourteen-hour day was a harsh reminder that my talents were not best rewarded in the field of stocks and bonds. So I entered college as a business major, thinking that something practical might provide well for a future family. Since I had an accountant for a father and two entrepreneurial grandfathers, a business career made sense.

But soon I fell under the influence of a wonderful, slightly enigmatic English professor who loved books and great literature. I quickly decided that if I were to heave garbage cans to pay for classes, I would spend my hard-earned tuition dollars on the most highly rated professors and best classes on campus. I decided to follow my heart, rather than the voice of practicality. From these passion-filled professors I began to find my calling.

The English and theology departments were my favorites. From old Dr. Sawtell I learned that our best mentors and life-time guides could be found in the characters of a well-written novel, and that a Shakespearean drama revealed human nature more clearly than a Myers-Briggs personality profile. Theology professors Dr. Baloian and Dr. Hartley introduced me to the great themes of Christian faith and some of the saints of the church. Dorothy Day and the Catholic Worker movement, Oscar Romero and his fight for the poor in Central America, Dietrich Bonhoeffer and his resistance to the Nazi regime, Oswald Chambers and his wonderful devotional material, and Mother Teresa and her work among the poor of Calcutta became my heroes and sources of inspiration. These people helped create a theological foundation by challenging me with a faith that was not simply an intellectual pursuit. Rather, faith was action.

And that's how I found myself at midnight on the doorstep of an apartment in a housing project in East Camden, trying to figure out what to do with Peanut.

Unfortunately, the lack of parenting would not be the only struggle my little friend Peanut would face as he grew up, for he lived in Camden, New Jersey—the second most dangerous city in America. Peanut would have to protect himself continually from violence. His school would graduate only 40 percent of its students and send less than 5 percent to college. The odds were against Peanut getting an education that would prepare him for adult life and a good job. And, with half of Camden's population under the age of twenty-one, Peanut would probably not find really good role models who would show him the right way. Since the city had little industry and few jobs for teens, the likelihood of Peanut resorting to selling drugs would be extremely high. The odds were stacked against Peanut.

Of course, I was committed to loving Peanut and providing the best day camp I could possibly create; but I knew deep down that this would not be enough to alter the circumstances of this young life. A summer of fun and frolic would be but a small blip on the screen of this young boy's life. There needed to be more—not only for Peanut, but also for the thousands of other children growing up in these circumstances. I began to ask some difficult questions. Could I just walk away at the end of the summer with my idealism intact—my insights about urban issues and my theology of the poor enriched—and add the experience to my resume? Sure, my volunteer efforts would look good on grad school applications. But could I continue to take advantage of all my privileges and just ignore the sense of responsibility I was beginning to feel for kids like Peanut? God was using this experience to begin altering the course of my life.

My experience that summer also challenged me to look at my faith a little differently. As I read through the Gospel narratives again, I was struck by the social implications of Jesus' teaching and his mission. While I was growing up in a Christian home, I always thought that my faith was about avoiding the deadly sins. You remember them: sexual immorality, impure thoughts, lustful pleasure, drinking, profanity, and such. Then one had to hold correct doctrines to get into heaven. But reading the biblical witness with a different set of eyes and a heart that had been broken, I saw that there was little mention of heaven in the Old and New Testaments, but a lot of discussion about the kind of world we are told to create. Whether I was reading the prophets Jeremiah, Amos, and or Micah or reading the words of Jesus, it became clear to me that God was concerned about the worldly condition of people—especially the oppressed, the poor, and those who have no voice. I could no longer read the Gospels without feeling challenged by a Jesus who committed himself to those whom society had forgotten and found of little value—the Peanuts of the world. After my summer in Camden I returned to finish my senior year of college. Then I returned to Camden for another summer of volunteer service. God continued to use those experiences to deepen my sense of calling, and, yes, I continued to pray for guidance.

When I returned for a third summer of volunteer service, friends and family began to get a little nervous. It appeared that I was not "outgrowing" my idealism. Parents and family were wondering when I would settle down. Friends who were beginning to scale the ladders of personal success would roll their eyes and ask, "Are you ever going to get a *real* job?" or "Are you ever going to work for a summer?" whenever I would call and ask for financial support. As they were interviewing for better jobs, with better stock options, I was begging them for donations so that I could pay for food and gas to take kids to the Jersey shore in the humid dog days of August. In their eyes, volunteering a summer to play midnight basketball with angry teens or coordinate afternoon softball games was something an idealistic young man might do once in his life—*not three summers in a row!*

With one foot in grad school and a host of people dropping hints as to what I should do with my life, I began to ask the questions: Who and what would determine my calling? The conventional wisdom of what a man is supposed to do with his life? Subtle peer pressure? The desires of family to see me find security and a stable job? Or should my calling come from spiritual convictions—the prompting of God's Spirit—and a growing sense that change for kids in the inner city would come about only if I were willing to establish roots in Camden and try to implement programs that would address the real issues those young people were facing.

I decided to drop out of grad school and start a year-round ministry in Camden. From that point my calling began to find definition and clarity. From my decision *to commit*, God began to expand my vision and show me the next steps.

How Do We Find Our Calling?

In the Scriptures, callings come in multiple ways. Some people hear a voice. Others obey a command. Still others just stumble their way into God's redemptive plan. Regardless of how this calling comes, one's calling seldom is crystal clear and detailed from the outset. Callings in scripture usually begin with a prompting from God's Spirit or a response of the heart. The prompting and our response are inevitably followed by *a risky step* or *an act of obedience* by the one being called. As the participant follows these God-inspired "nudges," he or she encounters difficulties and challenges, but ultimately one's calling becomes a little clearer.

The encounter between the Syrophoenician woman and Jesus is very helpful when we think about the question of a call. The story also shows a very interesting development of Jesus' mission and ministry.

Both Mark 7:24–30 and Matthew 15:21–28 reveal that Jesus had withdrawn into the district of Tyre and Sidon, a predominantly Gentile territory. While Jesus was in this area, he did not seek any mission activity among the Gentiles. There were moments of healing and teaching, but Jesus was not reaching out to the Gentile people. The passage raises a question: why was Jesus selective about whom he reached with his ministry and message?

A woman approached Jesus. It is important to note her background. She was both Gentile by race and Greek by culture. She was a "hellenized" person—someone who spoke Greek and was otherwise integrated into Greek culture. The designation also suggests the woman's socioeconomic rank; hellenized people were usually upper-class people. When this upper-class, Greek-speaking, Gentile woman came to a wandering Jewish, Galilean teacher and healer, two very different social worlds met.[12]

Josephus, the great Jewish historian, recorded that the inhabitants of Tyre were some of the bitterest enemies of the Jewish people. For many years the cities of Tyre and Sidon had oppressed the Jews economically and politically. The Galilean backcountry and rural areas around Tyre, where Jewish farmers could be found, produced most of the food for the city dwellers. But often the city dwellers bought up and stored so much of the harvest for themselves that in times of crisis the country farmers did not have enough. This created hostile and bitter feelings.

We read of this incredible encounter against this backdrop:

> A Canaanite woman from that region came out and
> started shouting, "Have mercy on me, Lord, Son of
> David; my daughter is tormented by a demon." But he did
> not answer her at all. And his disciples came and urged
> him, saying, "Send her away, for she keeps shouting after
> us." He answered, "I was sent only to the lost sheep of the
> house of Israel." But she came and knelt before him, say-
> ing, "Lord, help me." He answered, "It is not fair to take
> the children's food and throw it to the dogs." She said,
> "Yes, Lord, yet even the dogs eat the crumbs that fall from
> their masters' table." Then Jesus answered her, "Woman,
> great is your faith! Let it be done for you as you wish." And
> her daughter was healed instantly.
>
> Matt. 15:22–28

To many of us who like to keep Jesus locked in a Superman
concept, his response seems very shocking. After all, this is
Jesus—the man who loved everybody, the man who never had
a bad day, the man who was boundless in his compassion and
mercy.

Then there came a woman who cried out from the deepest
recesses of her heart, "Have mercy on me, Lord, Son of David;
my daughter is tormented by a demon." This was no flippant
request. She gave Jesus deference and acknowledged who he
was. But Jesus did not respond. Did he not hear her because of
a hearing problem?

Jesus' eventual response indicated that he did hear the
woman perfectly well. What Jesus' response reveals is that Jesus
had a certain view of what he was called to do. "I was sent only
to the lost sheep of the house of Israel." Jesus sensed a divine
responsibility to Jews but not to Gentiles. The calling Jesus
embraced for his life was defined by ethnic boundaries.

At this point one could hope that Jesus would have stopped
and said nothing further. I am almost embarrassed with his next
statement. It sounds so—well—harsh and out of character. "It
is not fair to take the children's food and throw it to the dogs,"
responded Jesus. It is clear that Jesus meant that the "children"
were the Jews, the children of Abraham. The "dogs" were the
Gentiles. Mark's version of the story seems to be a little softer—
a little gentler: "Let the children be fed first." Mark's account
seems to suggest that there is room for a Gentile mission *after*
the mission to the Jews, but Matthew's account suggests a flat
refusal.

At this point in the story, the Syrophoenician woman went head to head with Jesus and challenged his exclusive view. Jesus had to decide if he was really going to withhold his mission from the Gentiles. The woman challenged him to rise up to a new, ethnically broadened sense of mission and calling.

New Testament scholar Judith Gundry-Volf upholds this woman as someone who played a significant role in the life and calling of Jesus. Gundry-Volf marvels at the woman's way of appealing to Jesus:

> She does not appeal to any right. Jesus does not allow for any right of the Gentiles to the fruits of his mission, and she does not argue to the contrary. She accepts the position of "dogs" in contrast to "children." She cannot assume a position of strength over against Jesus. She is a woman, entreating for another woman, a double gender disadvantage in the context of male/female relations of the day. Even if she does come from a higher socio-economic status than Jesus, this is more a disadvantage than an advantage for her, since Jesus would presumably identify her with the oppressors of her Jewish neighbors. Her ethnicity, her gender, her socio-economic status—she can build on none of these things a case for Jesus' intervention.[13]

To what did this woman appeal to get Jesus to change his mind? She appealed to mercy, and this appeal touched Jesus deeply and caused him to rethink his mission. Gundry adds, "Yet, when the powerless woman impresses on him the power of mercy that is not based on privilege through birth or deserts, Jesus' sense of his mission is expanded through this principle of mercy, the basis of her faith."[14]

Because of this encounter, Jesus now expressed *compassion* for the Gentiles. The mission and calling of Jesus were expanded because of an encounter with another human being. This change of heart is further supported in the following verses (Matt. 15:29–39). Here we read of a Jesus who did not want to send any of the Gentiles away hungry. Whereas he initially denied "bread" to the "dogs," here he fed more than four thousand Gentiles with bread and fish. This is a dramatic turn of events.

Many people may have difficulties with this interpretation of Scripture. The very thought that Jesus could have changed, or was somehow restricted by the ethnic boundaries of his day, violates our picture of Jesus—the one who was perfect and sinless. But does having a limited understanding of one's calling have anything to do with not being perfect or *sinless*? Absolutely not. Part of being human is having limitations. We are limited people. God, as incarnated in the life of Jesus, embraced limitations. Sadly, instead of embracing the idea and learning from this life-changing encounter, many choose to spiritualize the event, saying something to the effect, "You know, Jesus was just testing the woman. He was going to help her all along." Or others might add, "Jesus knew that his mission was to both the Jews and Gentiles, it just wasn't time yet for him to expand his outreach. You know, God's timing."

This passage has tremendous implications for those who want to discover their calling. The passage says to me that God uses our encounters with people to direct and expand the intentions God has for our lives. Whether it is with a five-year-old boy named Peanut, with a college professor, or with a weak and vulnerable woman whose daughter is dying, these encounters can dramatically alter and shape our lives, if we allow them to.

This idea of vision and calling being birthed in us when we encounter other people—especially those with need—is articulated well by a young pastor named Matthew Barnett. He has developed a very large outreach ministry in Los Angeles called the Dream Center. His is a dynamic church that never closes its doors. In his autobiographical book *The Church That Never Sleeps*, Barnett states,

> As Christians, we may think that to get vision, we have to go to a mountaintop somewhere and wait for hours for a revelation about what to do with our lives. Or we may feel that we have to go to a camp meeting or revival center to find out our purpose. But nothing of what exists today at the Dream Center was born out of a *mountaintop experience*. All of the vision was born in the valley. You see, in the valley we are close to the need. It's the place where we see the hurt. Walking the streets, identifying with the people, and seeing the needs today started all of Dream Center's two hundred ministries. After we saw a need, a vision came to fulfill that need.[15]

Barnett's life and calling began to gain clarity when he ventured out among the people. He quickly realized that God uses people to *expand* vision and calling. His sense of calling and vision for his church did not come while he sat in his study preparing sermons, nor did it come during a worship service. Like many of us, Barnett was waiting for God to tell him what to do with his life. Little did he realize that God would speak to him through the people he met in his community.

A First Step: Giving the Whole Self

The question I am continually asked by Christian college-age students is "What is God's will for my life?" Without a doubt this is the most pressing question for a Christian who is about to graduate from university or college. To be nearing graduation without any specific plan can be frightening and cause tremendous stress. But it is not just a matter of making the right decision: Should I go to grad school? Should I work for a year? Should I take a year and travel? Should I get married? Beyond these very practical questions, there is often a very sincere desire to find God's plan for our life. But before we can truly begin to find the answer to this question, a first step must be taken.

Paul wrote to the church at Rome, "I appeal to you therefore, brothers and sisters, by the mercies of God, to present your bodies as a living sacrifice, holy and acceptable to God, which is your spiritual worship. Do not be conformed to this world, but be transformed by the renewing of your minds, so that you may discern what is the will of God—what is good and acceptable and perfect" (Rom. 12:1–2). In this passage of Scripture, Paul offered some basic first steps to finding God's will and calling for our lives. The first challenge the apostle gave to this group of believers was to offer their bodies as living sacrifices. Because of the mercy God had displayed in their lives, Paul called the people to respond. Paul was not laying a guilt trip on the readers or threatening them. Paul was appealing to the disciples in Rome to reflect on their unique experience with God. Karl Barth argued that the Greek for "appeal" means "comfort" as well. By exhorting them, Paul *strengthened* and *comforted* these Christians. He reminded these believers that as Christians they were continually embraced by God's mercy. This is the place from which we must start.

Paul then borrowed some vivid imagery from the Old Testament to communicate the extensiveness of this teaching. In the Old Testament, God's people offered different kinds of sacrifices to God for different reasons. There were "sin offerings," "guilt offerings," and "peace offerings." What these offerings had in common was that they usually involved some kind of gift—perhaps an animal—that was to be given to God. They were called *sacrifices* because they cost the giver something. In order for people to get right with God, they would have to give one of their *best* birds, *best* lambs, or *best* goats to the priest. God was not to be offered blemished sacrifices. Nor would partial sacrifices be offered. Never does one read of someone offering the leg of a goat or the wing of a bird. Offering a sacrifice carried the implication that the gift would be given to God *in its entirety*.

For people who were immersed in the culture of sacrifice, Paul's imagery would be difficult to misinterpret. When Paul called the church at Rome to bring their bodies as *living sacrifices*, there would be no mistake that Paul meant for people to lay their whole life down at the altar. For Paul, understanding the will of God and finding the will of God for one's life begins with surrendering every aspect of one's being to the intentions of God. The first step to understanding God's is letting go of everything we possess—our careers, our finances, our free time, our sexual lives—and offering our whole selves to God for the service of Jesus. Thus the Dutch theologian Abraham Kuyper captured the essence of Paul's exhortation when he claimed, "There's not one part of our lives that Christ does not exclaim, 'Mine!'"

Compartmentalization

Most of us, if we are honest, have difficulty embracing Paul's challenge. We love to compartmentalize our lives. We give God a half hour each day (on a good day), a tenth of our income, our Sunday morning, but we keep the rest of our lives to ourselves. We give God partial sacrifices and hang on to the things that we want to control. *My* desires, *my* dating life, *my* money, *my* thought life, and the way *I* entertain *myself* or govern *myself*. The "spiritual" stuff I give to God.

A few years ago my wife's grandmother was living with us. We called her Gramma Hall. Every Christmas her friends would send boxes of chocolates for her. Gramma Hall loved chocolate. I quickly noticed, however, that there were certain kinds of chocolates that she did not like—the soft ones. The hard chocolates she could suck on for hours. But for some reason she did not like the creamy soft chocolates with the marshmallow and liquid fillings.

Gramma Hall had a simple system to determine the difference between the soft and hard chocolates. She would take her thumb and press down on each of the chocolates. If the thumb made a dent in the chocolate, she moved on to the next until she found one that suited her. In the process she left behind the casualties of her experiment—half-full boxes of crushed chocolates.

One day I brought a cup of water and a few cookies to her room. As a token of her appreciation, she turned and offered me a box of her chocolates. I looked into the open box of chocolates. Sure enough, the remaining chocolates all had her thumbprints adorning their tops. Not wanting to hurt her feelings, I accepted the box of chocolates with a smile and a few words of gratitude.

As I carried out the box of chocolates, I had a good chuckle. Bless her heart. She really meant to give me something nice. Her intentions were good. But as I reflected on the incident, I was struck by the similarity between her gift to me and how I often give my life to God. So often I hold on to the areas of my life that I want to hold. Then I give back to God what is convenient. I give God my half-eaten box of chocolates.

According to Paul, when I experience the grace of God, I should respond by offering my whole life back to God. In the words of Eugene Peterson, we are to offer our lives as a "living present" to God. Only when we can truly say, "My life, my career, my future, my decisions, my dreams, and my entire all belong to God," are we on the road to discovering God's calling for our lives. When we can say, "God, you gave me this great education. Here, it's yours—it's yours to do with it whatever you want"—then we are close to becoming a *living sacrifice*.

A Second Step: Thinking Differently

Paul gave a second challenge to those of us who want truly to find the will of God. Paul's admonition to the church at Rome was, "Do not be conformed to this world, but be transformed by the renewal of your minds." Not only are Christians to surrender their entire lives at the altar of God, but Christians are to commit themselves to the transformation of their mind. In order truly to discover God's will for one's life, Paul believed that Christians need to think differently from those who do not hold to a Christian worldview.

A few years ago there was a fascinating study done on graduates from some of the major Christian universities and colleges around the country. Those students, graduating from schools that taught a biblical worldview, were compared to non-Christian students graduating from secular universities. Did the Christian students hold different views in the areas of vocational commitments, the kinds of jobs they take, what they would do with their money, the kinds of cars they would drive, where they would live, and whom they would marry? Surprisingly, the study found that there was very little difference between Christian graduates and graduates who did not profess Christ. What the study exposed was the fact that the faith of the Christian students had not permeated into their thought processes and worldview. The students had conformed to the patterns of the world.

Interestingly, George Barna contends that 25 percent of all Americans claim that their worldview is founded on biblical principles, yet less than one in ten is able to explain what this means. Furthermore, his study discovered that one out of three Christian adults *reads* the Bible. One out of ten Christians *studies* the Bible. Fewer than one in twenty-five memorizes any Scripture. Less than 2 percent practice all of these on a weekly basis. In addition to Barna's statistics about a lack of biblical knowledge, theologian Douglas Hall expresses his concern about the state of the North American Christian's ability to truly think Christian in his book called *Thinking Faith: Christian Theology in a North American Context*. Hall alerts us to the fact that there is a serious theological crisis in our churches and that "our faith, however heartwarming it may sometimes have been, has been lacking intellectual depth—in theology!"[16] Both Hall and Barna conclude that there is little mind transformation taking place in the lives of contemporary Christians. Our values and our thinking about God are being shaped by the dominant culture.

Later in Romans 12, Paul gave the reader a glimpse of what it means to think differently from the dominant culture.

A person who is *not conformed to this world*:

- Does not think of him or her self more highly than they ought to think
- Values the gifts of others in the body of Christ
- Loves others with mutual affection
- Is ardent in spirit
- Is patient in suffering
- Prays
- Extends hospitality to strangers
- Blesses those who persecute him or her
- Associates with the lowly
- Does not repay evil for evil
- Lives peaceably
- Overcomes evil with good

As you can see, this is not the wisdom of the dominant culture. Paul presents *counterculture thinking*. It is a worldview that is not controlled by the idolatrous powers of our age or the common sense of the surrounding culture. A transformed and renewed mind thinks differently. Thinking differently leads to a different kind of lifestyle—a lifestyle that is more in tune with God's will.

For people trying to find their life calling, Paul's words in the book of Romans offer an important and critical starting place. Total surrender of our lives to God, coupled with a commitment to thinking differently from the world, moves us to a place where we can hear more clearly the voice of God.

A Third Step: Knowing Yourself

One of the great challenges of life is to discover who we are as a unique creation of God. Each person on the planet is different. We have different personalities, different ways of learning, and different ways of perceiving the world. The great quest of life is to understand who we are as one who is made in the image of God. Understanding our uniqueness can be the beginning of discovering what we are called to do in this world.

As Os Guinness puts it, "A sense of calling should precede a choice of job and career, and the main way to discover calling is along the line of what we are each created and gifted to be. Instead of, 'You are what you do,' calling says: 'Do what you are.'"[17] Guinness's spin on discovering calling is somewhat counter to how many were raised. Most of us come out of the mind-set that we are to go to school, get a good job, and then allow that job to define our lives. Guinness believes the exact opposite. We are to discover who we are and then allow that discovery to shape our lives. I think Guinness's approach is consistent with what Scripture suggests.

Arthur Miller Jr. and William Hendricks pick up on this theme in their book *Why You Can't Be Anything You Want to Be*. They argue that our whole educational system is misguided because it ignores giftedness. Sure, the system rewards academic giftedness, but it does little to help individuals find their *personal* giftedness. "Today, kids are on their own when it comes to figuring out who they really are and what they have to offer," begin the authors. "The result is that most of them waste years of their lives, many thousands of dollars, and untold misery groping for an answer."[18] These authors go on to suggest that teachers should be helping their students understand what is unique and special about the way they learn and work—not just getting them to learn a bunch of facts so they can pass tests. "Giftedness cannot be taught or developed. Students arrive with their unique pattern already formed," they continue. It is the teacher's job to help students discover their giftedness.

Each year our ministry offers a one-year internship opportunity. College students and college graduates from all over the world come and spend time in the inner city of Camden, Wilmington, Vancouver, or Toronto working with children and teens. One of the reasons our leadership team is committed to this program is that it helps students and college graduates discover their gifts and their potential callings. Within the context of a Christian community, there is opportunity for young adults to begin to understand *themselves* and begin the process of reflecting on their *unique* and *special* talents and gifts.

Few students have really been affirmed in their uniqueness, and few students have any sense of what God has called them to do with their lives. Many have spent sixteen years in a traditional academic setting and still have no sense of what God is calling them to do with their lives. There have been few opportunities during their lifetime to connect classroom learning with their unique and special gifts and personalities.

What often happens in those internships is that students make a few discoveries about who they are. Some find out they are *not* called to urban ministry or working with children and teens. Their time of running outreach programs, tutoring at after-school sites, or coaching softball teams reveals to them that their hearts' desires and gifts are not best spent in this manner. Whenever an intern comes into my office at the end of the program and says, "Bruce, I've had a great year, but I just don't think this is my calling," I am delighted. They have discovered what is *not* their calling. They have responded to God's prompting and realize that urban youth work does not fit with their giftings. This is an important discovery.

Usually I ask these students some further questions, like "What aspect of the internship did you enjoy?" and "Describe some moments from the past year when you really felt alive and felt as if your gifts were being used." Often they describe events that gave them tremendous satisfaction and communicate stories of when their actions were received very positively by the community. These revelations are important clues for taking next steps toward finding their vocation. "I loved leading devotions—sharing the Bible with my peers was a terrific experience." This student has discovered that she has a passion to teach Scripture, and this initiates a journey toward theological study and seminary. "Helping a mother find child care for her daughter and discover her health care benefits was really important for me." This student has discovered that he really enjoys trying to connect resources with people and will move toward a degree in social work. I have heard the response, "You know, the health care in the city is horrific. Where are all the good doctors?" This student has discovered that her undergraduate premed degree has not been a waste of time. Rather, God can use her interests in medicine to help underserved communities. These students have one thing in common: their internship has allowed them to close some doors and yet leave with new revelations about themselves and what God might want them to do with their gifts.

Over the years I have seen interns go on to become schoolteachers, pastors, social workers, urban architects and planners, doctors, nonprofit directors, and entrepreneurs. Many of these students began to discover their callings by spending a year in a community that helped them find their God-given gifts and talents.

The Role of Community

Finding one's calling is not a solo enterprise, something done in isolation. Few of us find our calling on a mountaintop. Since part of finding one's calling is discovering what is special and unique about oneself, it is vital that we create relationships with people who know us and who have observed us in various contexts. Often we are blind to our own strengths and weaknesses. We need people in our lives who will be honest and point out gifts. We need people in our lives who will help us say no to the temptation of trying to do things that really are not consistent with whom we were created to be. This can be incredibly affirming and helpful. We quickly discover things about ourselves that we never knew. And that experience can save us from years of pain, low motivation, and apathy toward our careers.

A friend of mine once told me that he was offered the presidency of a university. This friend is a dynamic teacher, gifted writer, and motivational leader. It was no wonder that he was an attractive candidate for this important position. Fortunately his small support community took him aside and told him that he should say no to the offer. When he asked why they felt that way, they all agreed that what the position required was not consistent with his gifts. If he took the position at the university, he would be spending the majority of the time doing administrative tasks. Administration was not his gift. He would have driven the university into the ground and suffered a great deal of pain. His community of friends helped him to stay true to his calling.

I remember once participating in a workshop that was designed to help people find their spiritual gifts. I was asked to write down ten events that really gave me great satisfaction— events that energized me and filled me with a sense of passion for what I was doing. I discovered that each episode I recorded was a situation where my staff was performing in the area of their gifts. It was about Karen teaching a group of prekindergarten students. It was Kim directing a major Broadway production for our teenagers. It was Pamela motivating a group of high school students to clean out an abandoned building. What I realized in the exercise, and what I have learned my calling to be, is to be a leader who creates an environment where disciples of Jesus can use and exercise their gifts most effectively.

The absence of community during the young adult years can be extremely costly. Without people in our lives who know us, know how we work, know what makes us passionate, and know what zaps our passion for life, we will have a greater chance of getting on a road that leads us to a destination where we do not really fit. We need other brothers and sisters in our lives who truly know us. But it takes courage to let people into our lives. It is risky to open ourselves to the input of other people. Yet having a community of people in our lives is extremely important when trying to find our life direction.

If Jesus Were a Senior

One Sunday morning I visited a Sunday school class of thirty-somethings in an affluent, upwardly mobile community not too far from my home. Sitting in a circle were a few young lawyers, a soon-to-be doctor, a pilot, and a bunch of other professionals. I found the dialogue fascinating.

"Sometimes when I fly strawberries to the U.S. embassy in India, I ask, 'What I am doing with my life?'" shared the pilot.

"When I settle a divorce case I wonder how this fits into the work of God's kingdom," added one of the lawyers.

"I've gone to school for ten years, including med school, and I still wonder if I've done the right thing. I wonder if I have wasted my time," mused the third.

For the next half hour I listened to a group of young professionals lament about their lives and what they were doing with their time. How many of these people were really fulfilled? How many were really utilizing the gifts God had given them? Did they really assess their gifts and special talents before they made the decision to start down the road to fulfill their career? Did they think about calling?

I have trouble believing that Jesus wants anyone to arrive at the age of thirty wondering if he or she has made the right choice in their lives. I believe Jesus wants students in their young adult years to take some time, reflect, and try to listen to their own unique heartbeat. So often I see students who suppress their own desires, interests, and passions in order to please their family or buy into what the world deems important. They end up regretting these decisions later in life.

A Conversation with Jesus

"So what are you going to do?"

I knew who it was, so I did not take the time to turn. I continued to read the job board, ignoring my Friend peering over my shoulder. Work From Own Home, claimed one ad. Computer Programmers Needed, suggested another. Job Fair: Nobody Goes Home Without An Interview, claimed the third. So many opportunities.

"Do you want a job or a calling?" continued my Friend.

"What's the difference?" I asked, hoping for a little clarity.

"Anybody can do a job. A calling is something deeper. A calling is a way of living your life in a way that is consistent with whom you were created to be."

"What's that supposed to mean?"

"You are unique," continued my Friend. I liked the sound of that statement. "You have gifts, ways of learning, a certain personality, and a unique history. God wants you to be true to those aspects of your life."

By this time in the conversation the job listings were becoming less important. Sure they were jobs—some of them seemed to pay well—but none of them really connected with my heart.

"What do you think God is calling you to do with your life?"

"I'm not sure," I responded.

"Why don't you begin to listen and reflect and try to learn what God is calling you to do? Don't jump onto a career path right away. Put yourself in a situation where you can learn about yourself and how your gifts can be best used to make a difference in the world."

I knew my Friend was right. I wanted more than a job. I wanted a calling. I wanted to wake up each day and feel that my life's energy was being directed toward what I was created to do.

Remember:

Every call from God, whether into some dull line of paid work or into an excursion from such work, is a call into play—into *fun*, if you will. If you turn it into mere labor, or into a career, or into a way of making money, it will either blow up in your face or burn you out—or both.

Robert Farrar Capon

Reflections for Students

1. Describe what is unique about your personality, your history, your passions, and your interests. Are your studies leading you in a direction that allows you to use your unique gifts?

2. Do you have a sense of calling? If so, what do you think that call might involve?

3. Is there a place where you can spend a year, or summer, exercising your perceived sense of calling? If so, what would stand in your way to keep you from doing an internship for a year? If not, what might you do to find such a place?

4. Do you have a community of people whom you can talk to about your unique gifts? If so, who are they? If not, what might you do to find such people?

For the Leader

Have your students write down ten situations/events/activities in the past year when they really felt alive, energized, and full of passion. Ask the students to review the list to see if any themes emerge. What might these themes tell them about possible callings?

Meditation

Lord,

Help me to find a calling.
Help me to discover my uniqueness.
Help me to create a vocation that aligns itself with my gifts and
　　with your Spirit.

Protect me from wasting years of my life doing things that kill
　　my spirit.
Help me avoid those things that diminish whom I am created to
　　become.

Lead me to a community of people who will know me and be
　　your voice.
Open my heart and eyes to your Spirit.

Amen

Chapter 4

Healing Preparations:
Moving toward Wholeness

True and substantial wisdom principally consists of two
parts, the knowledge of God and the knowledge of
ourselves.

John Calvin, *Institutes of the Christian Religion*

People are born broken. They live by mending. The grace
of God is glue.

Eugene O'Neill

May I talk with you?" asked the young woman. The
chapel was slowly emptying of students who had just
participated in the worship service I had led.

"Sure," I responded. Since most the students seemed more
interested in getting to the cafeteria for lunch, I was encouraged
that *someone* had, perhaps, listened to my sermon and had a
probing question.

"What would you like to talk about?" I asked, in an effort to
begin the conversation. She hesitated, and didn't respond.

We sat down in the front row. I spoke again.

"How do you like the retreat?"

"It's good . . . good. I mean . . . I'm really enjoying myself."
I began to ask another question, but she interrupted. "I suppose
you want to know why I want to talk with you . . . but . . . I'm
not sure I can share it with you." She was looking at the floor
and cracking her knuckles. I decided to try to ease her tension
with a few safe questions about herself. Her name was Mia, she
was twenty, and she had been involved in church for many
years—in fact, she was a leader in the group and participated on
the worship team.

"What do you want to share with me, Mia?" I asked again.
By now the chapel had cleared out.

"It's too awful," she persisted. Now I'm not a trained counselor, but it didn't take a Ph.D. to figure out that she needed to
make some kind of confession. "Mia," I said as warmly as I
could, "What has you upset?" Tears rolled down her cheeks.

"I just feel so dirty. If anyone finds out . . . they would be
so disgusted . . . and I'm the worship leader. I feel like such a
hypocrite."

I waited. Mia slowly revealed the secret she had been har-
boring. "I can't help it. But it's just so . . . so disgusting. I'm
hooked on porn. I've tried to stop, but I can't, I don't. I rent the
movies and watch them when my parents aren't home. I'm hor-
rible. I feel so bad."

The chapel was silent. The tension and the stress she had
exhibited earlier had disappeared. She was not cracking her
knuckles now. Her secret had been revealed. "I can't talk to a
counselor. How could I do that? Where would I go? If anybody
found out, they would be shocked and so disappointed. I'm supposed to be the big spiritual leader."

I was surprised. Mia knew that there was a part of her life that
was out of control, but she did not feel that there was any safe
place to share her secrets. Even the promise of being anony-
mous with a counselor seemed a potential threat to her image
and reputation. Her fear of the shame of being discovered ham-
pered her from beginning to confront her problem. Each time
she gave in to another film, her guilt and self-hatred grew. Each
step backward enforced the belief that she could not escape the
guilt and the power of this addiction.

But this day, when she had confessed her ensnaring behavior,
she had taken a first step. I strongly suggested that Mia find a
good counselor and deal with this issue in her life. It was obvi-
ous that it controlled every aspect of her being—the way she
viewed herself, the way she perceived her relationship with
God, the way she related to other people. Her distorted sense
of sexuality had control.

What Should I Do?

It is axiomatic to say that there is a proliferation of sexual mate-
rials in our culture. Pornography is everywhere. Every time you
boot up your e-mail service, you have to delete a slew of requests
to visit various web pages offering everything from hot beastie
sex to incestuous sexual acts or a bunch of roommates getting

it on together—all mixed in with ads for low-interest bank loans, cheap ink jet cartridges, and new floor wax. Porn has become just one more commodity. Whereas a few years ago people would have to go out of their way to find sexually explicit material, now it is available literally at our fingertips, twenty-four hours a day.

Moreover, one can hardly flick through cable TV channels without being bombarded with sexually explicit images and offers for phone sex numbers. Movies also are increasingly graphic, especially movies for teens and young adults. Hollywood producers capitalize on mixing sex and violence in almost everything that comes to the big screen. Unless a person is totally isolated from the world of technology and media, it is difficult to be removed from their influence. Pornography and sex are big business.

Some argue that late adolescence and young adulthood are just times of "experimentation"—a time to sow wild oats! "Get it out of your system," is the popular psychology. "You'll grow out of it," come the voices of secular wisdom. So, before you throw up your hands and give way to the wisdom of MTV, see if there are any connections between behaviors in our early adult years and our later relationships.

Eye-Opening Facts

Consider these facts about the porn industry:

- On the Internet, twenty million adults visit cybersex sites *each month*.
- Pornography is one of the most profitable ventures on the Internet, with revenues increasing from $52 million in 1996 to more than $2 billion in 1999.[19]
- Young male adults are major targets.

Many Christians—not just students—naively like to think that if one just reads the Bible enough, spends enough time in church, and prays with holy vigor, they will find themselves above the temptations of the flesh.

In a sadly interesting article entitled *Tangled in the Worst of the Web*, Christine Gardner writes honestly about the increased number of pastors who are dealing with an addiction to pornography. If anyone is above temptation, shouldn't it be pastors? Gardner writes, "Experts say pastors—who, like many in positions of leadership, are isolated, under pressure to lead exemplary moral lives, and subject to intense on-the-job emotional stress— are at greater risk to become addicted to porn."[20] She goes on to cite a few more insightful reasons why those in positions of Christian leadership are more likely to fall into the trap of porn:

- Leaders are put on pedestals as perfect examples.
- Leaders can feel that their understanding of porn (I have to view it in order to understand it) will enable them to help sex addicts.
- Leaders can have a sense of justified entitlement (I am above the law).
- People of faith can wrongly convince themselves that their little academic dabbles into the world of pornography or sexually deviant behaviors will have little or no enduring impact on their faith and life.

The sad part of the pornography issue for students is that, too often, churches don't know how to deal with people who are struggling in this area. People can share about overcoming drug addictions, alcohol addictions, and eating disorders, but if that person—especially someone in leadership—mentions that he or she is dealing with a sexual addiction, usually he or she is ostracized and out of a job, with nowhere to turn, dealing with the addiction in isolation.

Before a student begins a career or starts down the road toward a lasting relationship, it is critical to address potential problems in this area and not ignore them. Behaviors that cannot be controlled will inevitably surface later in life. Even the most sincere Christian is misinformed or self-deluded if he or she believes that hiding in full-time ministry or a marriage will heal problems associated with addictive sexual behaviors. It won't. And sweeping problems under the rug only inhibits the process of healing. Inevitably the problem will express itself— and just when the stakes are highest and the cost is greatest. It can cost a marriage and mess up the lives of one's children. It may cost a position of leadership and hurt hundreds of people who looked to you for guidance.

If this is your struggle, be willing to expose your secrets and begin the process of healing. Realize that what is done in the isolation of one's private life has an impact on oneself and others. The problem with pornography, for example, is not simply what takes place in acts between people but the fact that it ultimately damages those people—people created in the image of God.

Karen A. McClintock writes, "We hear a lot about how pornography degrades women, but it also degrades men. While pornography promotes male fantasies of power over powerlessness, it also promotes self-destructive attitudes in men. By providing substitute gratification, it provides an escape for individuals seeking to avoid relating to their partners in fully human and respectful ways. Pornography also encourages unrealistic sexual expectations for both men and women."[21]

A Tragic Phone Call

My receptionist buzzed me. "There's a woman named Rita on the line." She had told our receptionist that she and I had attended college together and that she needed information on our ministry for a master's thesis she was working on.

It was twenty minutes to six, and I had promised my wife that I would be home for dinner. I picked up the phone promising myself to make the call very brief. We talked about the research she was doing for her master's program—something like faith-based social work (surely this could have waited till tomorrow!). Then the conversation took a dramatic turn. "Ya know, Rich left me and the kids?"

"What?" I was stunned.

"Yes, he left me and the four kids."

It couldn't be. Rich and Rita were the perfect couple in college. Both were deeply committed to Christ and were leaders on campus. Rita always had a smile and an encouraging word. Rich was one of the smartest students on campus and was always serious about his commitment. Rich took the most difficult theology classes and asked questions that kept the professors on their toes. He was the kind of guy who even read the footnotes!

They had gotten married when they graduated and then had begun to build their family. Rita homeschooled the children. The family was very active in their church. He had a good job.

"We didn't even have a television or a VCR," she said. "We just lived without it and thought nothing of it. Then Rich began going into the office a lot at night, and I was glad about his excitement about his job. But then I started seeing strange charges showing up on the Visa bill. At first I just ignored them. Then I decided to investigate"

Unfortunately, I knew where this conversation was going. I glanced at my watch. I was going to be late. Rita continued to pour out her heart. "I discovered Rich was heavily into pornography and would not admit that he had a problem. I finally decided that I had to leave. His behavior had become so erratic."

As she continued to tell me about his deviant behavior and the tyranny he imposed on her and the children, I heard the kids screaming in the background. Rita sounded frazzled, worn out, a mother afraid of her husband, yet trying to raise her children and protect them from potentially damaging behavior.

"The thing that really ticks me off"—Rita paused for a moment, took a deep breath—"he is teaching Bible studies at a new church. They love *him* and they think *I'm the weird one!* He's fully manipulated them into believing his story."

After I had hung up the phone, I just sat in my office chair and stared at the wall. Another family had been destroyed because of a sexual addiction. Another mother was left to create some stability in a home. After they had been married, she told me, the unresolved issues of Rich's childhood began to surface. He wrongly had assumed marriage would magically cure his problems. Sadly, it did not.

The cost of our hidden *secrets* is high. Part of preparing oneself for life—especially a life of discipleship—is having the courage to move toward *wholeness*. Whole and healthy people bear good fruit. Whole and healthy people have good relationships. Whole and healthy people bring wholeness and health to others—not destruction and chaos. Therefore, health begins with exposing one's secrets, which takes courage. It takes a willingness to look at oneself *honestly* and begin to take the steps needed to bring healing to one's life. It usually takes someone— a professional Christian counselor—to help.

Exposing the Secret: Why I'm Not Eating

Pornography and unhealthy sexual behaviors are not the only issues that impact the health and well-being of students. Young adults on campuses face additional pressures and challenges that can lead to a life of instability and brokenness.

In the spring of 1996 something strange began to happen in the kitchen of a sorority house at a large northeastern university. Hundreds of plastic sandwich bags began disappearing. When the sorority president began investigating, she soon found her answer. The bags, filled with vomit, were hidden in a basement bathroom. To her disgust and surprise, she also learned that the building's pipes needed to be replaced because of erosion caused by gallons of stomach acid.

"Yet in a way it all made sense," she said, for most of her forty-five housemates were terribly worried about weight. "It was like a competition to see who could eat the least. At dinner they would say, 'All I had today was an apple,' or 'I haven't had anything.' It was surreal."[22]

This is not an atypical scene at colleges. In 1999 it was estimated that five to ten million females and about one million males suffered from eating disorders. Marcia Herrin, codirector of Dartmouth College's Eating Disorders Education, Prevention, and Treatment Program, contends that those who suffer are generally young (14–25), white, affluent, and perfectionist, type-A personalities. According to Seattle's Eating Disorders Awareness and Prevention group, an estimated 5–7 percent of America's 12 million undergraduates are afflicted with anorexia (a pathological fear of weight gain, leading to extreme weight loss), bulimia (bingeing followed by purging) or binge eating (compulsive overeating).[23]

Sadly, people at risk deny the problem or avoid getting help because of the stigma attached. It's their shameful secret. But the shame becomes debilitating. In a poll of student health-care professionals at the country's 490 largest colleges and universities, 39 percent said that *denial* is the biggest hindrance to treatment.

When asked why disordered eating is so common among college students, Dartmouth College's nutritionist Marcia Herrin wrote, "College is a time of major change. Students are suddenly on their own with food, usually for the first time in their lives, and often they gain weight and then diet, which triggers eating problems."[24] Herrin goes on to say that "it may take a long time for kids to recognize they're suffering from an eating disorder . . . they worry about the stigma attached . . . they may worry that college administrators will find out, or they may be afraid of their parents' reactions."

Christian students trying to live out their faith can suffer even greater depths of pain than their secular counterparts. Too many times I have heard young adults languish in the guilt of "disappointing God," or "If only I had a stronger faith," or "I keep sinning." A distorted belief in God can add to shame and stress. Sadly, the church—or the family of faith—is not always the place where a struggling sister or brother can find help and healing. "What will the pastor and the deacons think of me?"

says the college senior. "Obviously I'm not a good Christian if I'm struggling with these issues."

An eating disorder is simply a symptom of a deeper issue—like a distorted view of God or a distorted view of one's self—so those who struggle with such issues must try to find the deeper source of their struggle. One young woman, who struggled with an eating disorder throughout high school and college, put it this way:

> As the eating disorder takes over, this extreme thinness appears to be ultimate control; but what it is really is a way to proclaim one's pain without acknowledging or expressing anything. The idea of being *not skinny* is frightening because it means a loss of identity. If I'm not skinny, what am I? If I'm not skinnier than everybody else, how am I different and special? If I can't keep losing weight, what *can* I do? If my weight and crazy eating habits don't scare people away, they might try to get to know me. If I don't have control of the food I eat, what do I have control of? And if I don't look sick, will you know how much pain I'm really in? How else can I tell you that everything isn't OK?

For my friend Susan, an eating disorder was a shield that kept people away from really knowing her. Her eating disorder also became a way to get attention in a distorted, unhealthy way. Being extremely thin was a way to stand out. Whether it was to keep people away or to get attention, there was a deeper struggle taking place in her life. There were issues of identity and issues of control or fears of a lack of control that needed to be resolved.

Although Susan is now finishing her last year of medical school, she does confess that overcoming her disorder has been far from easy. She continues by sharing:

> Feelings of inadequacy and unworthiness are themes that have kept popping up in my struggle with an eating disorder, as well as in my spiritual walk. Had I not begun to deal with these issues in college, I think they would have been much worse after college. College for me was a little bit like being in a little pond; it was easy to find a niche and excel. In the years after college, while out in the real world, I've been surrounded by people who are smarter than I am, went to better schools, are more well-traveled, are more well-read, are better dressed . . . the list goes on! Had my self-worth been built upon my accomplishments, personality, or body, it would have crumbled quickly. I've

had to revisit the truths that I learned while I was recovering from my eating disorder again and again, this time in a more ruthless environment. I found counseling to be extremely helpful in dealing with all of these issues; ideally, a Christian counselor can help make some of the spiritual connections and help a person understand how God can heal you.

Susan's story is encouraging because it reveals that there is hope and possibility of healing. Susan is a testimony that a person is not destined to live in the bondage of an eating disorder for their entire lives. With help, with friends, with a loving a supportive family, with good counseling, and with a healthy perspective on God's love, healing can take place.

What Does a Person Do?

Over the years I have seen young women working in our youth programs who have suffered from eating disorders. What they all have had in common was that they suffered *in secret*. They vomited when no one was home or in the isolation of their dorm room. Only after they were caught did they begin to talk about their problem—if they did begin to talk. Only after the secret was exposed could they begin to take steps toward wholeness.

Frederick Buechner reminds us that "we are as sick as our secrets," but "to get well is to air those secrets if only in our own hearts."[25] He cites an ancient church prayer that reads, "Almighty God, unto whom all hearts are open, all desires known, *and from whom no secrets are hid*; cleanse the thoughts of our hearts by the inspiration of thy Holy Spirit, that we may perfectly love thee, and worthily magnify thy holy name; through Christ our Lord. Amen." The prayer reminds us that our secrets are not hidden from God. No matter how hard we try to *repress* or *deny* or *pretend*, God knows what is going on in our hearts. Thus, there is no point being ashamed or embarrassed. God already knows. Secrets are hidden only from other people, not God. And our secrets exist only because we are unable to look honestly at ourselves and then have the courage to ask others to help us in the healing process.

However, exposing our secrets is easier said than done, for it can be one of the most difficult things we ever do. The author of the best-selling book *The Road Less Traveled*, M. Scott Peck, uses different language to describe what needs to take place. Peck calls everyone to a commitment to a life of truth and responsibility. This kind of commitment calls for a "life of continuous and never-ending, stringent self-examination."[26] Peck believes that few people are committed to living this kind of life, because it is to painful. Truth and honesty with oneself are a challenge because they call us to take responsibility for those things we would rather not face. "The reason people lie is to avoid the pain of challenge and its consequences," writes Peck. Therefore, exposing these aspects of our lives cuts against the grain of what is natural for us as humans. But Peck adds sarcastically, "It is also *natural* to defecate in our pants and never brush our teeth." We *can* overcome our natural tendencies to lie and protect our public self-image.

Pornography and eating disorders are vivid illustrations of behaviors of people who were not willing to look honestly at their lives, expose their secrets to a trusted friend or professional, and face the challenge and pain of overcoming the addictions. Mia had carried her secret for years before she shared it with me. She lived with a painful lie. Fortunately, she made a first step toward healing by breaking the spell of her secret and continued to seek help. Rich, however, as of this writing, still lives his lie. Not only has he not confronted the demons of his past, he spreads lies about his wife to deflect attention from himself.

Forgiveness—Usually Part of the Process?

Once our secrets are exposed, however, and we begin to deal with some of the causes of our addictive behaviors, forgiveness plays a significant role in healing. Our unhealthy behaviors can be connected to our inability to forgive—whether it is a neglectful parent, an abusive sibling, an overcontrolling mother, or someone who has hurt us deeply. Over the years I have been impressed with the courage of individuals who have finally forgiven those who have hurt them.

Twenty-three-year-old Darlene Jones was one of those people. I was teaching a class of college students. The subject: forgiveness in the Bible. Little did I anticipate that the class would become a place of confession and healing for the students. After sharing some Scripture and insights from research done by social scientists on the significance of forgiveness, I asked the students if any had experienced the benefits of forgiveness, *firsthand*. After a few minutes of uncomfortable silence, a young woman to my right spoke up.

"I was not dieting but losing weight," shared Darlene. "I had lost fifteen pounds and wasn't sleeping—I was a real mess and on a downward spiral. It was about a guy." I had always seen Darlene as a very self-confident, *together* twenty-three-year-old. As she began to tell her story, the other students were transfixed. Although they had lived in the same house and worked together for the previous six months, there was obviously a lot about her life they did not know.

"Finally, my mother pointed out to me what was going on. I was in a relationship where I was deceiving myself that everything was OK. I was in denial and played it out by not eating."

Up until that point in the class, I had talked only a little about the physical effects of forgiveness. I had tried to bridge the abstract with the reality of how forgiveness has a profound impact on a person's physical and emotional well-being. But I wanted the students to move beyond their intellectual assent to a few Bible verses about forgiveness to a place where they looked at their own lives more carefully. Darlene's vulnerability was opening the door for God's Spirit to move. "Finally, I faced the facts and went to the guy and said, 'I forgive you.'" Darlene chuckled, "Of course he didn't know what I was talking about, but it was a significant turning point for *me*. I started to get well again."

The group was mesmerized by her openness and willingness to be vulnerable. Others in the group began to share freely. Testimonies of forgiveness began to flow. Some shared about people they had forgiven; others shared about how they still were hanging on to past hurts and wrongs. Unable or unwilling to forgive, they carried their burdens for years. What the evening illustrated for me was how infrequently people are given the chance really to open up in a safe place, a place where they will be encouraged and find acceptance. For an hour and half those students created *community*—a safe place where they could talk freely and look more closely at their lives.

One of the most radical aspects of our Christian faith is this wonderful practice of *forgiveness*. The practice is the heart of our faith. It begins with God forgiving and embracing us—regardless of what we have done—so that we, in turn, can forgive others.

As Christians we are often quick to accept the forgiveness of God, and we expect to be forgiven for our wrongs. And yet too often, when it comes to forgiving others, the forgiveness comes slowly and reluctantly . . . or sometimes not at all. That's why the Lord's Prayer has always intrigued me. "Forgive us the wrong we have done, as we have forgiven those who have wronged us," taught Jesus in Matthew 6:12 (NEB).

Immediately following his prayer, in verse 14 and 15 (NEB), he continued, "For if you forgive others the wrongs they have done, your heavenly father will also forgive you; but if you do not forgive others, then the wrongs you have done will not be forgiven by your father." Jesus put it clearly. If you don't forgive others, God will not forgive you! For many believers this concept does not sit well. We have come to expect that all a Christian is called to do is ask God for forgiveness. We fail to see that our forgiveness of others is just as critical.

So why did Jesus place such emphasis on the practice of forgiveness? Because forgiveness initiates the healing process of past wrongs and hurts that have been committed against us. Lewis Smedes, who did some ground-breaking research on the subject in the early 1980s, believed that there is tremendous personal benefit to forgiveness. Smedes wrote that "untold pain is brought about in the world by people's unwillingness to forgive and the corresponding passion to get even."[27] Without forgiveness we will live a life of unresolved anger and bitterness.

The unresolved issues will surface in other areas of our life and affect our behaviors. Robert Enright, another social scientist who has researched the issue of forgiveness, offers some helpful ideas when going about the process of forgiveness.

1. One must make a conscious decision not to seek revenge or nurse a grudge but instead to forgive.
2. One must formulate a rationale for forgiving. For example: "By forgiving I will experience inner healing and be able to move on with my life."
3. One must accept the pain one has experienced without passing it off on others, *including the offender*.
4. One must extend goodwill and mercy toward the offender, wishing for the well-being of that person.
5. One must realize the paradox of forgiveness: as one lets go and forgives an offender, the offended will experience release and healing.[28]

The capacity to forgive another human being is a wonderfully therapeutic gift from God. Our ability to forgive will lead us further down the road toward wholeness—toward the place God desires us to be.

If Jesus Were a Senior

Personal wholeness is that wonderful image of what we are supposed to be as God's people. We were not designed to be broken. We were not created to be angry and bitter. We were not put on this earth to perpetrate our brokenness and hurt others. As whole persons we are to bring health and vitality into our relationships. As whole persons we are to be agents of God's love and grace—in the world and in our communities and families.

But the concept of wholeness begins with Jesus. Frederick Buechner articulates this vision of wholeness wonderfully in his book *The Longing for Home*. Buechner writes, "It is in Jesus, of course, and in the people whose lives have been deeply touched by Jesus, and in ourselves at those moments when we also are deeply touched by him, that we see another way of being human in this world, which is the way of wholeness."[29] Buechner goes on to say: "When we glimpse that wholeness in others, we recognize it immediately for what it is, and the reason we recognize it, I believe, is that no matter how much the world shatters us to pieces, we carry inside us a vision of wholeness that we sense is our true home and that beckons us."[30]

Buechner argues that from this sense of wholeness we find a deep sense of peace, the peace that Jesus offers. As we move closer to the fullness of Christ, we discover an inward peace that has nothing to do with what is going on around us. Buechner claims, "His peace comes not from the world but from something whole and holy, because deep beneath all the broken and unholy things that are happening in the world, Jesus sees what he calls the Kingdom of God."[31] This is an incredible gift, the gift of peace that allows us to turn away from the destructive behaviors that lead toward brokenness.

The intent of this chapter has not been to provide solutions for destructive behaviors but, rather, to encourage you to look honestly at your life. Too many of us carry secrets. Too many of our friends carry secrets that never get confronted; we incorrectly assume it is not our business to bring a word of truth to them. We have seen that without acknowledging and dealing with our problems, untold destruction and pain result. How great it is to be assured that God knows our innermost secrets and still loves us passionately and deeply. Nothing we can do will squelch the relentless love God desires to give us.

Take courage. Repent. Seek help. Break the power of your secrets, and find support from those who are wise and full of God's love and grace.

A Conversation with Jesus

"You know, it's funny."

My dorm room was absolutely dark. I was alone, just having a few moments of meditation before I closed my eyes for the night. Conversation was the last thing on my mind.

"What's funny?" I asked reluctantly.

"People." It seemed odd to hear that coming from my Visitor. I thought he liked people.

"They have it all wrong," continued the Voice. "First, they think they can hide from me. They do things in the solitude of their rooms, their bathrooms, the seedy bookstores, or at their computers. Oh, maybe they're ashamed. But they think I don't see."

This was about the last thing I need to hear at 10:00 P.M. I began to think over the past few weeks. What had I done? I was about to be confronted by my unexpected Guest.

"But they've got it all wrong," he continued. "They think I'm out to get them. They think that the bad stuff they're doing annoys me. It doesn't annoy me. It saddens me. It saddens me because it diminishes them from becoming whom they were created to be."

"Wha'da'ya mean?" I asked.

"Well, each of us was created to be a loving, healthy, passionate, joy-filled person who has the capacity to build rich, life-giving relationships. Everyone has the potential to evolve into a beautiful masterpiece. Instead, they fill their lives with tawdry junk and become like a gaudy velvet painting that hangs on a cheap motel room wall."

For the next few minutes I sat in silence. I thought about the statement.

"I think I get it," I responded slowly. "The issue isn't so much what I can get away with without getting caught; the issue is that my unfortunate, Spirit-defeating behavior leads me farther and farther away from what I was created to become."

"Now you're getting it," responded the Voice. "And the best part is that I want to help. I don't want people to be bogged down by their secrets and live in shame. I want them to discover freedom and wholeness. Secrets are deadly until they are exposed. And, joyously, they lose their power when they are brought to the light."

"This helps," I replied. "Yes, this makes sense." I closed my eyes and drifted off to sleep.

Remember:

We must try to discover the real person we are, otherwise we cannot encounter the Lord in truth. From time to time something authentic shows through. . . . At these moments we see something of the true person that we are. But no sooner have we seen than we often turn away because we do not want to confront this person face to face. We are afraid of him (or her); he puts us off. Nevertheless this is the only real person there is in us. And God can save this person, however repellent he may be, because it is a true person. God cannot save the imaginary person that we try to present him, or to others or ourselves.

Anthony Bloom

Reflections for Students

1. How pervasive is pornography on your college or university campus? Do you think it is a problem?

2. Besides sexual addictions and eating disorders, what are other addictive behaviors students deal with on campus?

3. How do you feel a person should deal with behaviors that are unhealthy and ultimately damaging to both themselves and others?

4. If you know a friend is struggling with some kind of addictive behavior, how should you respond? If you are in a relationship with someone who is struggling with some kind of addictive behavior, how should you respond?

5. How are you taking steps toward wholeness?

For the Leader

It might be good to divide men and women into separate groups to talk about these issues—you might find a deeper level of honesty. If appropriate or possible, it may be best to have someone who has struggled with destructive behaviors—and has over-come these behaviors—facilitate the groups. Also, have some resources available for your students, e.g., counselors or books that can help students who desire to grapple with these issues.

Meditation

Lord,

I desire to be a person who brings life, love, and peace into the
world.
I desire to develop healthy relationships with others—
relationships that build others up and not break them or
me down.
Grant me the courage to look honestly at myself.
Help me to be truthful in my self-examination.
Grant me the courage to expose my secrets, so I can find healing
and liberation.

And Lord, give me grace for the journey.
Help me to believe that you can heal—that you will heal.

Amen

Chapter 5

Pacing Preparations:
Holy Walking

To consider persons and events and situations only in the
light of their effect upon myself is to live on the doorstep
of hell.

Thomas Merton

Jesus *stopped* . . .

Mark 10:49

The Transforming Power of Being Noticed

Our youth gospel choir had finished an exhilarating performance at a church about an hour outside the city, and
we were on the way home. The kids were sprawled across the
van seats as we chugged our way down the highway. Troy, however, was sitting on the edge of his seat, eagerly talking with our
choir director.

"That's going to be *my* testimony one day, too, Mr. King!"
said sixteen-year-old Troy.

"What do you mean?" replied our weary director.

"Well, you said that you were shy and did not have much confidence as a kid."

"That's right, Troy. You've got a good memory," Mr. King
said, in his encouraging baritone. But before he could utter
another word, Troy cut him off.

"You said that somebody *noticed* you and *encouraged* you to
develop your gifts as a musician. You said that your life changed
after somebody *noticed* you. Well, that will be my story one day,
Mr. King."

I kept my eyes on the road as I guided the van through the
freeway traffic. But I was musing on Troy's story. Eight years ago
Troy, then seven years old, had been wandering the streets of
South Camden—one of the toughest sections of our city. Little

80

Troy happened to bump into one of our college volunteers who was recruiting kids to come to a neighborhood day camp. That was the beginning of Troy being *noticed*. Over the next years staff workers gave lots of time to Troy, whether it was teaching him to sing, tutoring him after school, or taking him out for ice cream on his birthday. Troy was being noticed by caring, loving adults. It transformed his life.

People Who Stop

After I got all the kids delivered back home, I began to reflect on my own life and those important, significant people who have influenced me. There is a common thread that connects them all: *they noticed me.* They were people who stopped, gave me time, and gave me attention. A college professor, a Sunday school teacher during my high school years, a mentor who came alongside me as I developed into a young professional—all these people shared a common trait; despite their busy and demanding schedules, they gave me the most precious gift, the gift of time. They were people who *stopped*.

And Jesus—our role model—stopped, too.

In the Gospel of Mark, Jesus responded to a blind beggar who was crying out from the side of the road. The man's name was Bartimaeus. Mark's recording of the interaction reads:

> They came to Jericho. As he and his disciples and a large crowd were leaving Jericho, Bartimaeus son of Timaeus, a blind beggar, was sitting by the roadside. When he heard that it was Jesus of Nazareth, he began to shout out and say, "Jesus, Son of David, have mercy on me!" . . . Jesus stood still and said, "Call him here." And they called the blind man, saying to him, "Take heart; get up, he is calling you." So throwing off his cloak, he sprang up and came to Jesus. Then Jesus said to him, "What do you want me to do for you?" The blind man said to him, "My teacher, let me see again." Jesus said to him, "Go; your faith has made you well." Immediately he regained his sight and followed him on the way.
>
> Mark 10:46–50

As I meditate upon this passage of Scripture, I find myself contemplating the character and life of Bartimaeus. I wonder what it would be like to sit on a dusty road day after day, year after year under the hot Middle Eastern sun. What would it be like to sit in total darkness with no light, no images, and no colors?

Surely he heard the travelers laughing, the children screaming, the mothers yelling, and the lovers whispering as they
passed along the road. He overheard the merchants talking
about their business deals; he knew the going prices of camels
and what commodities one should invest in with one's extra
income. But it was frustrating to live continually in dark isolation and aloneness.

Bartimaeus could *feel* those who busily passed him by—not
that anyone would ever stop to touch him. He felt the dust stick
to his face each time an entourage or wagon passed; he felt the
gravel and dirt spray against his legs by the wooden wagon
wheels and scuffling feet.

Thinking about Bartimaeus and trying to put myself in his
place, I have to wonder if he ever grew resentful. Did he ever
resent the sound of coins tinkling against the rocks in front of
his little wooden bowl? Perhaps he was thankful for those who
felt pity, but he could deal with a little hunger—*in exchange for
the touch of another human being.* He longed for conversation and
laughter and relationships.

I wonder if Bartimaeus ever muttered to himself, "If only
someone would stop and notice me. If only someone would see
me as a human being and stop to ask a question."

Mark 10:49—one of those overlooked and underappreciated
verses in the New Testament—reports a radical event: that *Jesus
stopped.* In essence, God stopped. The Creator of the universe,
incarnate, in human flesh, stopped. The most significant person
ever to walk the face of the earth stopped.

The importance of Jesus' action is heightened by the fact that
he had just announced to his disciples his impending death. "We
are going up to Jerusalem," he said, "and the Son of Man will
be handed over to the chief priests and the scribes, and they
will . . . kill him" (Mark 10:33–34). His earthly life was coming
to a close. Time was short. *Yet Jesus stopped.* Not only did he stop,
Jesus stopped for a man who could do nothing for him. He
stopped for a man who could not prolong his life in any way or
add to his waning popularity. But Jesus took the time to stop.

If I were in Jesus' shoes, sensing that my death was imminent,
I would be asking the question, "How can I really maximize the
time I have remaining?" I would be filling my Day-Timer or
Palm Pilot, trying to squeeze out every last minute so I could be
as effective as possible. If I were in Jesus' shoes, I would be asking the disciples to set up rallies so I could preach my last sermons to as many people as possible. I would be asking my

disciples to keep their pencils sharp to record as many of my last words as possible.

But Jesus did the opposite. He made a statement with his life. Against the background of an impending, ugly death, Jesus provided a snapshot of what it means to live authentically. He gave time and attention to someone who was a *nobody*. By providing this image of Jesus, Mark challenges us to see that part of our responsibility of living as disciples is to be *people who stop*—people who can step back from the hectic pace of the world and stop for the lost and lonely.

Addicted to Hurriedness

Richard A. Hoehn, in his book *Up from Apathy: A Study of Moral Awareness and Social Involvement*, tells of a fascinating study done of students attending Princeton Theological Seminary. Forty seminarians were asked to give either a short talk about the parable of the Good Samaritan or a talk comparing ministry with other occupations. The students met in one building on campus, but then were instructed to go to another building to deliver their talk. On the way to their appointments the students encountered a man in a doorway. The man was slumped over, with his head down and his eyes closed, and he was not moving. As each seminarian passed, the old man coughed and groaned. The primary focus of the study, yes, was to determine whether those on their way to talk about the Good Samaritan would be more likely to help a distressed person slumped in a doorway.

There was an additional variable introduced into the research—the degree of hurriedness. The first group of students was told to hurry right over to the auditorium because the program was running late. The second group was simply told to be prompt. The third group was told they had a few minutes until they were due at the other building.

The conclusions of the research were fascinating. The content of the talk did not really matter; the subject had little influence on the behavior of the person giving the talk. *What mattered most was the degree of hurriedness.* A person in a hurry was unlikely to stop. A person who had extra time was more likely to stop and help. Ironically, some of the seminary students going to give the talk on the Good Samaritan literally stepped over the victim.

Reflecting on the results of his study, Hoehn asked a question: Since the degree of hurriedness makes a significant difference between response and no response, can individuals who live in the midst of a culture that drives people towards hurriedness actually live a life that can "stop" and respond to various situations in a moral manner? Hoehn believes that society needs to change in order for individuals to respond with greater faithfulness.

In a less stressed, less frantic, and less driven world people are more likely to stop and respond to those in need. But we also have to be realistic. The majority of us are going to be living and working in a world that is addicted to speed, performance, and results. Most of us will not choose to live some kind of radical lifestyle that sets us apart from our culture—like the Amish or alternative communities. Therefore, is it realistic to think that we as Christians can live in a way that is not totally controlled by a frantic lifestyle? Can Christians live in the world and not be consumed by the dominant behaviors of the world? It is difficult. But just as we can choose between eating junk food and eating healthier foods, between watching good movies and watching bad movies, we can choose to take steps to create a "life pace" that makes our stopping more probable. The first step, however, is to realize that a pace of life that does not allow us to really notice or respond to what is going on around us is not the way God wants us to live.

Thomas Merton, a Catholic monastic who spent his life trying to balance contemplation and activism, criticized the hurried nature of contemporary culture. Merton believed that overactivity is actually a form of violence against humanity. He writes that "to allow oneself to be carried away by a multitude of conflicting concerns, to surrender to too many demands, to commit oneself to too many projects, to want to help everyone in everything, is to succumb to violence."[32] In short, Merton says that modern life—a life that is often marked by a continuous need to succeed, acquire more, and live on the edge—is actually a violent life. It is a violent life because it destroys the capacity for real inner peace. It destroys the capacity to stop and notice what needs to be noticed.

Patricia Pearson, a freelance writer, has another conclusion when it comes to an overcrowded, busy life. In a *USA Today* article called "Rage! We're a Culture on the Verge of Losing Control," Pearson points out that we "are a culture on the verge of truly losing it . . . we are living with an unbearable amount of uncertainty about everything in our lives, from the trivial stress of which of 65 channels on TV to watch to the profound dilemma of what direction to take in a radically changing corporate world."[33] This uncertainty and busyness of the mind,

Pacing Preparations 85

contends Pearson, releases itself in different kinds of rage—road rage, office rage, hockey-dad rage. The list goes on.

I think Pearson is correct in her conclusion, but she falls short when limiting the sources of rage to simply living in a world of increased uncertainty. Overactivity also feeds rage. Motorists stuck in traffic, having to meet a deadline, are filled with rage. Moms and dads driving their children from one activity to another are filled with rage. Employees given impossible deadlines and goals for the sake of company profits are filled with rage. Rage is the result of overactive people living in a world of increased uncertainty.

How Do We Cultivate a Jesus Pace?

The "secular" world is not the only culture living at a high-speed pace. God's people too often have bought into the notion that godliness is somehow connected to busyness. Pastors are often busy, overstressed people. Our Christian heroes are flying around the country being busy people, trying to keep impossible schedules. In many circles hurriedness is not only an acceptable Christian practice; it has become the mark of an "on-fire" spiritual life. With hurriedness being modeled in every corner of the Christian community, how do we begin to develop a lifestyle that cuts against the grain of contemporary culture, allows us to live at a pace that gives more time for God's Spirit to move, and allows us to be people who *stop?* Here are a few ideas that might help:

Sabbath

A few years ago I heard a sermon that helped me look at the concept of Sabbath in a whole new light. The preacher was doing a series on the Ten Commandments. His point was clear. "If I commit adultery," he began, "I will lose my job." The nods of the congregation affirmed his statement, as if they were saying, "You've got that right. And don't try it, buster!" He continued, "If I kill somebody, I will be put in jail." Again, nods from the congregation. "If I covet the latest sports car and use my salary to live with extravagance, I will be criticized for living too lavishly." At this point in the sermon he paused and said, "But . . . if I break the Sabbath, I will be rewarded and admired for my hard work." No one in the audience nodded. "Why," the pastor asked rhetorically, "is breaking the Sabbath not considered a sin?"

Keeping a Sabbath in our lives is not some legalistic ritual designed to cramp our lifestyle. The idea of Sabbath is a gift to us. Sabbath allows us to break the addictive cycle of hurriedness—a lifestyle pattern that easily envelops our lives. Every time we keep the Sabbath, we allow ourselves to counteract the pattern of the world and establish a pattern of life that is modeled on God's intentions for creation.

Let me put it another way. I have a problem with chewing my food—I really do. For some reason I did not listen to my mother when it came to this area of my life. If I do not think consciously about chewing, I tend to swallow before the food is ready to be swallowed. Once in a while I find myself gasping for air and reaching for a big gulp of water. My dinner gets stuck in my throat, and I cannot get it to go down the pipe. I have eaten too fast. I did not pause. Perhaps this is an overly simplistic analogy, but just as I forget to chew my food, we can become so busy that we never take the time to really chew on life—we just keep shoving in one more event, one more appointment, one more crisis after another.

Eventually this lifestyle will catch up with us. Just ask someone who has had a nervous breakdown or anxiety attack. Developing a Sabbath rhythm to our life is a little like the discipline of pausing between bites of food. Sabbath allows us to chew on our life for a bit—to think and reflect about how we are living our lives and what God is trying to teach us. It allows us to reflect on the moments we have failed to stop for those by the side of the road.

Sue Klassen takes this concept of Sabbath keeping and adds a creative twist. In an article called "Our Sabbath Year,"[34] Klassen talks about an exercise she incorporated into the life of her family. She asked the question, "What if we spent a year just not acquiring anything that's newer, faster, easier, prettier, more sophisticated, longer lasting, better, or—that most empty improvement—*the latest*?" What Klassen wanted to do was break the cycle of consumption that had begun to control the life of her family. "It encouraged us to break free from the accelerating cycles of consumption and allowed us to choose contentment—a rest from more and better." This idea of the Sabbath year helped Klassen create a pattern to her life that allowed space for stopping. It broke the cycle of franticness that so often drives us from one activity to the next—not allowing us to become *stoppers*.

Sabbath is not attending church, and church is not a substitute for Sabbath. In fact, church involvement can feed the addiction of hurriedness and add more events to an already overcrowded schedule. Overcommitment at church can actually hinder us from really being sensitive to God's Spirit and noticing hurting people outside the doors of the church.

A friend of mine was recently attending a big mission conference that attracts more than 30,000 people over a weekend. Zealous Christians attend this conference to learn more about missions and about making a difference in the world for Jesus. There are great workshops and the best speakers. People are motivated and challenged to go "into all the world" and share the Good News. Well, my friend was on her way into the conference one day when she was approached by a homeless man. He asked her for some spare change to buy something to eat. Rather than giving the man some change, for fear he would buy liquor, she asked him if he were hungry. Yes, he told her. So she took him to a fast-food restaurant and bought him dinner. On the way, the man said, "Ya know, I've been out here all day asking people to give me some change for food. Most people don't even stop—don't even look at me. You're the first to stop."

When my friend heard this, she was absolutely livid. "Can you believe it?" she angrily told me the next day, "All those Christians going into the conference to hear about missions and ministry, yet nobody would even stop and give that poor man the time of day. What a joke! We want to think about meeting Jesus in some far-off land, but when we meet him on the street, we walk right past him."

Her critique cut right to my heart. All of those Christians were in a rush to hear the next speaker or the next Christian band and participate in the next workshop. Their Christian conference was just one more event in their already frantic lives.

Sabbath is not church. Sabbath is not the next conference or the next concert. Sabbath is reflection, solitude, a time of inactivity—a time when we can slow our hurried selves down. Developing the behavior of Sabbath is critical if we want to live life at a "Jesus pace."

Retreats

One of my favorite activities in college was visiting a local Catholic retreat center that was a few miles from my campus. The wonderful gardens, the well-stocked library, and the hospitable priests made it a wonderful Sunday afternoon getaway. Just to spend a few hours walking the garden trails and meditating on the Stations of the Cross was enough to slow me down and help me refocus my life. Those miniretreats showed me the value to stepping away from the hectic schedule of writing papers and studying for exams. They showed me how to step away from people and service, to reconnect with God. Those short retreats taught me the importance of *stillness* and *quiet*.

Unfortunately, now I do not have a wonderful Catholic retreat center a few miles away from my home where I can visit on a Sunday afternoon. But what I do have is the memories of those short retreats and the important role they played in my life. Consequently, I still strive to build *miniretreats* into my life today. My brief respites momentarily release me from the sharp talons of a culture that is addicted to stress and overactivity. I have found that if I want to walk at a Jesus pace, I need occasional retreats to remind me that I can walk at a pace that allows me to stop.

There are all kinds of spiritual retreats we can incorporate into our lives. There are silent retreats—times of contemplation and prayer. There are study retreats—times when one can break away for a few days and really think about a particular issue. There are retreats that are led by others, and there are retreats that we can lead ourselves. Most important, it is critical to occasionally break away from the normal routine of life and take time to pause and meditate.

Reflection

Here's an exercise that will help you to become a person who walks at a Jesus pace: spend some time at the end of each day in silent reflection. Ignatius called it the Examen of Conscience. Basically, Ignatius encouraged his disciples to spend ten minutes each evening meditating upon the events of the day. Ignatius reviewed each of his encounters, each conversation, each meal, and each moment, asking a simple question: "Was I open to God, who was there for me?" This exercise teaches us to reflect upon how we spent our day and how we responded to the situations that God put in our path. The purpose is not to fill our self with a sense of failure and self-contempt, but rather to learn how to live more intentionally for God in the midst of ordinary life. As we review our day like a slow-motion movie, one frame at a time, we begin to see opportunities where we could have *stopped* and invited God into the situation or circumstance.

Again, we learn to live more intentionally, more aware of what is taking place in our midst.

The late Catholic writer Henri Nouwen talked about a wonderful concept called "the portable cell." Nouwen believed that a Christian could develop a discipline of being able to enjoy solitude and reflection even in the midst of a crowded, busy life. Rather than having to go into a "cell" to pray, Nouwen argued that a person could imagine him or her self in a "cell" on a subway, in the shopping mall, or at a baseball game. Even in the midst of crowded places, Nouwen felt he could go into his cell and have a time of reflection and solitude. He could meditate upon his life and think about what he was doing. He could "pray without ceasing."

Nouwen told of a time he was in his study at Yale Divinity School, working feverishly on a book. There was a knock on the door. He opened the door and found a student who wanted to talk. Instead of inviting the student in and listening to him, he shooed the student away so he could get back to real ministry—his books. When he went back to his studies, he meditated for a moment on the situation and was struck by what he had done. It was then, said Nouwen, he realized that *interruptions* were his ministry. Nouwen began to change his life. He began to view unexpected knocks on the door and phone calls as opportunities to stop and share God's love and compassion. A reflective life enabled Nouwen to change his way of thinking and alter his priorities. Unfortunately this concept is easier said than done. It takes tremendous discipline to engage in introspection and evaluation each day.

Sabbath, retreats, and reflection are a few behaviors that will help disciples build into our busy lives a life rhythm that allows us to be more attentive. Cultivating these behaviors can help us to become more like the stopping Jesus of the Gospel narratives.

Why the World Needs "Stoppers"

A number of years ago, when the late Mother Teresa came to America, a reporter followed her around. At one point the reporter asked this saint, who had worked for years in the horrific poverty of Calcutta, how the poverty in America compared with the poverty in Calcutta. Her answer surprised the reporter. She claimed that the poverty in America is much greater than the poverty in Calcutta. "It is the poverty of being nobody to anybody," she responded with great insight.

Our images of poverty include people sleeping in cardboard boxes under freeway overpasses or children walking across a desolate sand dune, half naked with bloated bellies. Seldom do we see poverty as a state of "being nobody to anybody." Mother Teresa broadens our view of poverty. Her definition expands our idea of what it means to be truly poor. If we embrace this definition of poverty, we quickly realize that the poor are not too far from us. The poor are those who sit by the side of the road and call out—both audibly and silently—"Somebody, anybody, have mercy on me." Our country is full of people like Bartimaeus—people who suffer from the poverty of loneliness.

Nobody to Anybody

Recently I said to my class of sixth-graders, "On the piece of paper in front of you, please draw me a picture of your best friend." I was teaching in one of our after-school programs and decided that I wanted to learn a little more about the students in my class.

For the next twenty minutes the children worked feverishly on their papers. With the class ending in a couple of minutes, I asked the students to put their crayons away and show me their drawings as they headed for the door.

Eric showed me a picture of his best friend, Peter. Tyshema boastfully displayed a picture of her sitting on her grandmother's knee, drinking a cup of hot cocoa. Jacob showed me a picture of his big brother playing football with him. Child after child came to the doorway to show me their beautiful pieces of art.

As little Michelle Torres made her way to the door, she passed me her picture and began quickly to exit.

"Michelle," I called her back, "I thought I asked you to draw me a picture of your best friend." The picture on her 8½" × 11" piece of paper was of a television set. I was sure that Michelle had misunderstood the assignment.

She paused for a moment, looked at me, and replied with total sincerity, "Mr. Bruce, this *is* my best friend."

My eyes were opened at that moment to a new reality. I realized that under the preadolescent smiles in my class, there were lonely kids—kids who just wanted to be noticed, accepted, and loved. I realized that our country is full of children and teens who believe that they are *nobody to anybody*.

A number of years ago a few researchers at Harvard University decided to see how much "quality interaction" took place between children and their parents in the course of a given day. These researchers attached tape recorders to each of the family members who were in the study to record what took place between the parents and their children. The researchers discovered that on average there was less than thirty seconds of meaningful dialogue between parents and children each day. Children were growing up in isolation, without significant interaction with parents.

One only has to remember the Columbine High School killers of a few years ago. The parents of the two boys had no idea what their sons were planning or what was on their minds. Furthermore, when they discovered their diaries, they realized that all the boys wanted to know was, who would buy the movie rights to their massacre. Would it be Spielberg or Tarantino? In essence, who would make them immortal? Out of their loneliness they craved attention.

In our inner cities, gangs are commonplace. Sadly one must ask: Why do kids join gangs? Kids join gangs because they do not want to be *nobody to anybody*. In the isolation of poverty and social chaos, kids can find a sense of identity and belonging only within the context of a gang. Their anonymity is replaced by a pseudofamily that provides attention and care. They become *somebody to someone* in a gang.

There are thousands of people like Bartimaeus across the country, crying out, "Somebody have mercy on me!" And tragically there are too few people traveling at a Jesus pace to hear the cries—and fewer who respond by stopping to notice.

Report Card Day

I sit in my office on the corner of Thirty-sixth and Federal Streets and watch the children come skipping up the sidewalk toward our tutoring center. I know it's report card day because as the children come, each with a book bag strapped to his or her back and a lunch pail in one hand, with the other hand each is waving the yellow slip of paper back and forth.

Why do they have these slips of paper out before they even get to our center? Because when they enter the doors, caring adults will take the time to read their report cards. And those adults will do a little dance and give hugs and high fives when they see the Cs that have been raised to Bs and the Bs that have been raised to As.

I remember one of those days very vividly. I was sitting at my desk working on a fundraising letter. I glanced up to see eleven-year-old Poncho leaning against my door jamb. Sure enough, he had a yellow slip of paper hanging from his right hand. I pretended not to notice. But he persisted. "What's up, Poncho?" I asked, raising my eyes from the computer screen.

"Nothin'."

Now I have worked long enough with youth to know that "nothin'" means they want you to keep asking. "Poncho, what's that in your hand?"

"My report card."

"Oh, can I see it?" He paused and tried not to reveal his smile. "Sure!"

As I looked at the report card, I saw that he had improved his Ds to Cs and his Cs to Bs. He had moved up in every category. Underneath the bravado, he was reeling in pride.

"May I make a copy?" I asked, knowing full well that he would not resist. He just nodded. I ran down to the photocopier and made a couple of copies. When I got back to my office, I gave him a big hug and congratulated him. I went back to my work, assuming that Poncho would head back across the street to our after-school program. Ten minutes later, when I emerged from my office, guess what? There was Poncho leaning against the office door of our accountant.

And for the rest of the day, all Poncho did was go from one office to the next, showing off his report card. Why? Because with a mom who worked two jobs and a father he had never known, Poncho just wanted to be noticed.

The people in our offices who stopped made a difference.

If Jesus Were a Senior

Thomas Merton wrote that "to consider persons and events and situations only in the light of their effect upon myself is to live on the doorstep of hell."[35] Merton believed that if we notice, talk to, spend time with, socialize with, and go to church with *only* people who can *do something for us*, we are living on the doorstep of hell. Our relationships become a series of social connections that we create to benefit . . . ourselves. This subtle self-centeredness moves us closer to a kind of hell. Why? Because we become the center of our reality; our center is not God and not others. Jesus did not consider people because they would make *him* feel better about himself or advance *his* social standing.

The temptation of becoming successful people is that our human relationships can become just a means to an end. We can *use* people. We can find people who help us advance *our* lives. Hence, we do not have time for "unimportant" people—people like Bartimaeus—who call out from the side of the road. We become people who are always looking over the shoulder of the person we are talking to—looking for someone else who is more interesting, more connected, better looking, more successful. Jesus contradicted this kind of lifestyle. The life of Jesus calls the disciple to develop a pattern of human conduct that allows for the care and attention for those who can provide *nothing* for us—those crying out, "Somebody have mercy on me!"

A Conversation with Jesus

"I've been watching you again."

I glanced over my shoulder to see who was sitting in the booth behind me. Pressed against my left ear was my cell phone. I was trying to coordinate a late-night study session with my biology partner. In my right hand I held a tuna fish sandwich that was dripping mayonnaise on page 180 of Bronte's Jane Eyre. *I was trying to get a few minutes of quality study time before my 1:00 P.M. exam.*

"Can I call you back?" I asked my friend and shut off my phone.

"Can't you see I'm a little busy?" I abruptly commented to my unexpected Guest.

"That's what I've been seeing."

"Wha'da'ya mean?" I asked with some agitation.

"You're living way too fast." Unfortunately I knew he was right. I was way overcommitted—involved in far too many activities.

"What's going to happen when you get out there in the real world?" he probed. "If you keep living at this pace, you'll never be able to hear me— you'll never see me. In rushing from one thing to the next, you're going to pass by a lot of opportunities to share my love."

"I never thought of it that way," came my reply.

"Begin to pace yourself. Take some time to think about your life, what you're doing, where you're going. Pause once in a while. Become aware of what is going on around you."

"But how? I feel like I have to be productive all the time."

"I know. That's the American way. But remember, your value does not come from your accomplishments. Your value comes from the fact that you are loved unconditionally, regardless of what you accomplish."

"So it's okay to take an afternoon off once in awhile."

"It's necessary."

"Thanks."

"Remember," said my departing Friend, "one of the great gifts you can give another is the purity of attention."

Remember:

When Jacques Ellul, the French theologian and social philosopher, asked people who took the speed train from Paris to Lyons what they were doing with the time they saved, he reported that no one was ever able to give him an answer. Ellul observed,

> The time saved is empty time. I am not denying that on rare occasions speed might be of use, for example, to save an injured person. . . . But how few are the times when it is really necessary to save time. The truth is that going fast has become a value on its own. . . . The media extol every gain in speed as a success, and the public accepts it as such. But experience shows that the more time we save, the less we have. The faster we go, the more harassed we are. What use it is? Fundamentally, none. I know that I will be told that we need to have all these means at our disposal and to go as fast as we can because modern life is harried. But there is a mistake here, for modern life is harried just because we have the telephone, the telex, the plane, etc. Without these devices it would be no more harried than it was a century ago when we could all walk at the same pace. "You are denying progress then?" Not at all; what I am denying is that this is progress![36]

Reflections for Students

1. How might you prepare to become someone who has the capacity to "stop"?

2. What kinds of preparations are you presently building into your life?

3. Do you believe that Sabbath is an outdated practice? How do you celebrate Sabbath?

4. Have you ever taken a silent retreat? Could you spend twenty-four hours in silence?

5. What do you think you might learn from the experience?

6. How can you give people in your life "the purity of attention"?

For the Leader

Ask your students to block out "stopping" times in their week—times to reflect, times to be still, times to give people "the purity of attention," times to observe Sabbath. Ask the students to share their experience the following week. Was it difficult? Why was it difficult? Are your students addicted to hurriedness?

Meditation

Lord,

I confess my need to be busy.
I like to feel useful. I like to feel productive.

I also confess how I use busyness as an excuse—
So I won't have to stop, or get close to others, or really look in
   the eyes of another.

Help me to become more like Jesus.
Help me to notice people who need to be noticed.
Help me to become a person who stops.
Teach me what it means to walk at a holy pace.

Amen

Chapter 6

Success Preparations:
Mustard Seed Conspiracies

We can not do great things,
only small things with great love.

> Mother Teresa of Calcutta

Servants or Superstars?

There was no knock on the door. A tall, thirtysomething man strode into my office, immaculately dressed in crisp khaki shorts, expensive sandals, and a yellow shirt embroidered with a polo player.

I was miffed that he had invaded my office and landed on my couch with no consideration for what I was doing.

"I've got to talk with you."

"Umm . . . sure," I responded with some hesitation. I could tell he was more than a little irritated. He was a youth leader from a large church in Florida. He had brought sixty suburban high school kids to our inner-city ministry for a work project. Each summer we host numerous groups of students who help with our day camps and do some repairs, painting, and gardening chores—things that we cannot afford to hire professionals to do.

He started right in. "We thought when we made plans for this mission project that we were going to do something important, something . . ."—he paused for a moment scratching his two-day-old beard—". . . something *big*."

I wanted to fire back, but I held my tongue.

"I mean," he sputtered on, "we could be pulling weeds, picking up trash, and painting just as well back home." He continued with a quiver in his voice; I thought it best to let him continue. "My kids were hoping that they could build something. I mean, do something that we could take a picture of—you know—sign our names on a plaque. The folks back home who supported us will want to know that their money really made a difference."

I listened patiently, I hope courteously, to this young leader for the next fifteen minutes while he talked about how he wanted his group to do something big, something *relevant*, something for the *needy people* they had come to serve. He wanted to make sure that his kids left the experience feeling good about their service—feeling like they were a success. He certainly didn't want them to leave with the feeling that they had *wasted their time*.

The humorous irony of the situation was that his spoiled teens from wealthy Florida suburbs could not even pull weeds with any degree of proficiency. Left alone to do even the smallest of tasks, his group quickly degenerated into complaints and whining; consequently, I wondered how this disillusioned leader could even dream that his group could manage to build something "big." Yet his group believed that their task was to do something relevant and important, cloaked in the disguise of helping the poor.

Of course, their intentions were misguided, starting with my brash young intruder. Sure, the heart of the Gospel had been misunderstood. Their misguided definition of biblical success did not align itself with the heart of Jesus.

The Mustard Seed Conspiracy

It is critical for the aspiring disciple to ask, What is *significant success*, personal importance for an individual who wants to live an authentic life? Or, to put it more directly, How did Jesus define success? To grapple with these questions before one gets too far down the career road is important. As a friend of mine once said, "I have watched people climb the ladder of success, only to realize when they get to the top that they were leaning against a building in which they had no interest."

Twenty years ago the author Tom Sine wrestled with the concept of biblical success in a book called *The Mustard Seed Conspiracy*. Part of the motivation behind writing his book was Sine's belief that unfortunately, perhaps unwittingly, the Christian community had bought into the dominant values of American culture. We equate success with power, prestige, and *big*. Sine reminded Christians that when Jesus shared the parables of the kingdom he "let us in on an astonishing secret. God had chosen to change the world through the lowly, the unassuming, and the imperceptible."[37] Successful people, according to Sine, were not the powerful and important; successful people were people who were part of what he called the *Mustard Seed Conspiracy*.

Throughout his book Sine writes about Christians who are engaged in unassuming, imperceptible acts in the most unlikely places. Sine gave his readers examples of people who embraced the vision of Jesus by moving into a slum and being a good neighbor, visiting children in a cancer ward, or opening their home as a gathering place for people of different ethnic or religious backgrounds. Sine's challenge was for *all* Christians to begin planting the imperceptible seeds of God's kingdom— seeds that the world would never notice.

One vivid example of his *conspiracy* was the impact a group of college students had on a man who became a significant political figure: Senator Mark Hatfield. Hatfield wrote in the foreword of Sine's book,

> Being a victim of *The Mustard Seed Conspiracy* through the faithfulness of a sophomore student at Willamette University, where I was dean of students, I have seen what God can do through faithful people. The students at that time had faith to believe that my life could be used by God to affect people throughout the State of Oregon. Little did they know that my life would . . . touch the lives of members of Congress, ambassadors, and Presidents, as well as others who aren't so well known.

Hatfield's life was changed by a group of students who got together every day to pray for their dean. Slowly, over time, Hatfield's heart began to change. The prayers of a group of college students made a difference. Hatfield went on to become one of the most outspoken, respected, and truly Christian senators of our time.

Jesus and Little Things

But it is Jesus who captures our imagination. If anyone in the history of the world could have done "big" things, it was Jesus. With his ability to heal, perform miracles, and draw big crowds, Jesus could have capitalized on the big. He could have built cathedrals, set up schools dedicated in his name, written books, possessed countries. Power was offered by the devil with seductive temptations. Instead, when Jesus talked about ministry, he talked about it in small, nonflashy terms. When his life and sayings are all boiled down Jesus redefined what it means to live a *truly successful life*.

For example, when he talked of God's presence in the world, Jesus used the metaphors of *mustard seeds* and *yeast*. He presented the idea that God's kingdom does not replicate the kingdoms of the world. God's kingdom is not about military might, it is not about the accumulation of wealth, and certainly it is not about jostling for political position and power. The reign of God that Jesus described starts small, like the mustard seed, and grows. Jesus reinforced his teaching by living out the principles in his own life. Instead of trying to speak to huge crowds, Jesus invested the majority of his time in twelve common, everyday, working-class men. Sure, there were moments when Jesus stood before crowds. But according to the Gospels that was not where Jesus invested his most energy. Jesus spent most of his life sharing and modeling true faith for a few people. In fact, the totality of Jesus' ministry can pretty much be summed up in the lives of his disciples. These were not big people—they were not the movers and shakers of first-century Palestine. They were, some thought, *nobodies*. They were not scholars—they were not even very good students. But they had a great teacher. Success for Jesus was when he poured his life into those *little* men.

Viewed against the conquests of Napoleon or Alexander the Great, the political popularity of J. F. Kennedy, or the tragic influence of Hitler, Jesus' investment in those twelve Galilean men was nothing but a blip on the time line of history. Napoleon conquered the continent. Kennedy sent a man to the moon. Hitler plunged an entire world into the carnage of war. Even though Jesus never traveled a hundred miles from his birthplace, his investment in these twelve men revolutionized the course of human history!

Interestingly, the life and ministry of Jesus were about doing *small things*. Although Jesus could have been seduced to build on his success, he resisted the temptation. Instead of building a traveling road show around his ability to perform miracles, Jesus told the recipients of his miracles to keep a low profile. "Tell no one!" he instructed those healed by his touch. While many contemporary Christians would take that kind of power and build an empire around it—all in the name of God, of course—Jesus downplayed the extraordinary things he was doing. Jesus understood that God's presence in the world was to be expanded through small but authentic acts of service—through imparting the ways of God into the hearts and minds of other people.

Even just before he died, Jesus did more *small* things. At the last supper he did the seemingly insignificant and humbling task of washing his disciples' feet. When many of us would have been planning more opportunities to get out and share our stories, or write down all our profound thoughts, Jesus was scrubbing the mud off the feet of his best friends. It was from his act (in the eyes of the world) of total insignificance that Jesus started down the path to Golgotha. At Golgotha Jesus' three-year ministry ended, and he died the uncelebrated, shameful death of a criminal—on a trash heap outside the gates of the city. And to top off his brief human life, Jesus looked down from the cross and saw only one of his disciples standing by his side. The rest were gone—afraid and maybe even huddled in a dark room back in Jerusalem. At his death there were no parades, no dignitaries, no twenty-one-gun salute, no media coverage, no monuments erected in his name. Jesus died the death of a criminal.

The residents outside Jerusalem probably said—at his death, if they bothered to notice at all—that Jesus' life was an irrelevant failure. Can't you just hear the skeptic saying, "OK, so he did some good things for people, taught some interesting ideas, and was faithful to his convictions. Sure, these are good things, but certainly nothing earth shattering."

But Jesus' measurement of success was not the same as the world's measurement of success. His measurement of success did not include numbers of people who "got saved," nor did it include the kinds of people he fraternized with, how he died, or any popular opinion poll. Jesus' measurement of success was motivated by love, truthfulness, and integrity.

Yet, stunningly, in Jesus' faithfulness and obedience to God he enters into the most significant event in the history of the world—his resurrection. And at the moment of the resurrection, Jesus' lifetime commitment to small things takes root in the minds and hearts of people and is transformed into something so expansive that the world has been reeling ever since. Jesus' teachings, lifestyle, and Spirit continued to live on in the disciples as long as they lived, and then in the early church in its shaky beginnings, and then it spread like wildfire. Jesus' life may not have been *successful* in worldly terms, but there has been no life in history that has had a greater impact.

Successful vs. Fruitful

In an anthology of his writings called *Finding My Way Home: Pathways to Life and the Spirit*, Henri Nouwen is quoted as saying:

What is your title? How much money do you make? How many friends do you have? What are your accomplishments? How busy are you? What do your children do? But it is important for us to remember that as we grow older our ability to succeed in this way gradually diminishes. We lose our titles, our friends, our accomplishments, and our ability to do many things, because we begin to feel weaker, more vulnerable, and more dependent. . . . Do we dare to look at weakness as an opportunity to become fruitful? Fruitfulness in the spiritual life is about love . . . and it is very different from success or productivity.[38]

Nouwen raises an important theme when we're thinking about the issue of success. Do we want to invest our life energies in pursuing things that eventually are going to elude our grasp? Do we want our bookcases filled with trophies and awards that will eventually lose their shine? Or do we want a life that is fruitful—a life that touches and changes other people and reproduces itself for future generations? Nouwen's challenge, as is Jesus' challenge, is to think hard about where we place our time and efforts, to think through our life commitments and our measurements of success—before it is too late.

This idea of true success is discussed in another wonderful little book called *Tuesdays with Morrie*, a dialogue between a dying college professor and one of his former students. The student, Mitch Albom, had been enamored of a certain professor, Morrie Schwartz, during his years at Brandeis University. But after university, Mitch lost touch with Morrie and slowly lost sight of life's meaning and forgot some of the values and lessons he had learned from this sage whom he had loved so dearly in university. Providentially the two became reconnected when Morrie began slowly dying from *amyotrophic lateral sclerosis* (ALS)—a brutal, unforgiving illness of the nervous system. Mitch began to visit Morrie every Tuesday and recorded their conversations. Mitch's life slowly began to find meaning again. One day the two men found themselves talking about success and money.

"We've got a form of brainwashing going on in our country," Morrie sighed. "Do you know how they brainwash people? They repeat something over and over. And that's what we do in this country. Owning things is good. More money is good. More property is good. More commercialism is good. *More is good. More is good!* We repeat it—and have it repeated to us—over and over until nobody bothers to even think otherwise."

Morrie was just getting warmed up. He had more to share on the topic.

"Wherever I went in my life, I met people wanting to gobble up something new. Gobble up a new car. Gobble up a new piece of property. Gobble up the latest toy. And then they wanted to tell me about it. 'Guess what I got! Guess what I got!'"

After presenting the problem of our contemporary culture, the aging professor provided his analysis: "You know how I always interpreted that? These were people so hungry for love that they were accepting substitutes. They were embracing material things and expecting a sort of hug back. But it never works. You can't substitute material things for love or for gentleness or for tenderness or for a sense of comradeship. . . . Money is not a substitute for tenderness, and power is not a substitute for tenderness. I can tell you, as I'm sitting here dying, when you most need it, neither money nor power will give you the feeling you're looking for, no matter how much of them you have."[39]

At this point in the dialogue, Mitch began to look around Morrie's house. He found that there was nothing new in the house. The TV was outdated; there was no CD player, just an antiquated turntable, and the furniture was all old. But what this young man did notice was the love that filled the house. There were friends who dropped by. The family was strong. There were honesty and open communication. Although the home had nothing of what the world would deem "success," the home was filled with love. *Morrie was a wealthy man*—he had far more than millionaires who lived in palatial estates with the latest luxury car in the garage. Morrie closed out this dialogue with a particularly poignant observation.

"Devote yourself to loving others, devote yourself to your community around you, and devote yourself to creating something that gives you purpose and meaning."[40]

What is a successful life? When you are lying on a bed dying from some horrific disease, what really matters? Is it the car in the garage? Is it the position you attained with your company? Is it the size of your stock portfolio? In the end, none of this *stuff* makes a difference. It does not satisfy our most basic human needs—the need to be loved, the need to have a vibrant faith, and the need to have lived a life of no regrets. Therefore, if we spend our entire lives sacrificing relationships and faith development—just so we can consume things we do not really need—we will die empty and alone.

Success in the Eyes of Jesus

Steve, a friend of mine, directs a ministry that is committed to those dying from AIDS. He's one of the most loving and caring people I know. Few people are more gifted in pastoral care. For me, the difficulty in his ministry is that there is no future to what he does, no success. Those with whom he works have no hope of recovering. *They will all die.* Steve helps them through the death process. Furthermore, he earns little money from what he does. There are no opportunities for success; no one gets better. Yet he has performed acts of selfless love—in the name of Jesus—365 days a year for the past ten years. He embodies the truth of biblical success. His small acts of mercy and kindness, filled with great love, capture and reflect the heart of God.

Let me share a story as an example of what he does.

The warning sign flashed "Respiratory Precautions" outside the intensive care unit. Behind the double doors lay forty-nine-year-old Ralph Currey, gasping for breath despite the help from oxygen tubes.

Ralph looked frightened, tense, and somewhat uncomprehending. As a late-stage AIDS patient, he knew that his days were numbered. Earlier that morning he had coughed up blood. Realizing that death was just around the corner, Ralph had asked the nurse to call Steve and ask him to come and sit with him during what could be his final hours.

While many Christian ministries focus on guiding new believers to lives of promise, Steve just tries to make the process of dying less fearful. "What happened?" inquired Steve as he entered the room and secured Ralph's mask.

"I coughed up some blood this morning," whispered Ralph. He wanted to be home, he wanted the needles gone.

"You look pretty scared."

Ralph paused a long moment, then said haltingly, "I've . . . put everything . . . in . . . the Lord's hands."

"You know, Ralph, we can commit things to God and yet still feel scared. That doesn't change our emotions."

"Well, I guess I *am* a little scared," replied Ralph.

Ralph was continuing to weaken. Steve just sat beside the bed, trying to be the presence of Christ for a man dying in isolation.

"Would . . . would . . . you rub my feet?" came a whisper.

Steve gave an assuring smile to Ralph and began to rub his friend's feet. As Steve described this act of ministry, he told me that he began to feel an intense narrowing of his focus, as if time was suspended and nothing else mattered. The task, according to Steve, took on a spiritual significance in and of itself. The room became filled with a heightened sense of peace and calm; there was an unmistakable sense of God's presence in the room. That small, insignificant act of rubbing a dying man's feet took on a sacramental quality. The spirit of God entered the room. Ralph experienced God's love through the hands of Steve.

When Steve got up to leave the room, Ralph reached out and caught Steve's hand.

"Thank you . . . thank you," he said softly. Ralph's face had lost its tense look.

I can hear the cynic say, "So, what's the big deal? I want to do something relevant with my life, and that surely ain't it!" But that's the voice of our self-centered culture—the voice of our self-centered religion—that has little to do with service and humility. As young disciples it is important for us to realize that *what we do* is less important than *how we do it*. As Mother Teresa said, "We do not do great things, just small things with great love." The wonder of that *Jesus principal* is that God is mystically found in the small things. I wonder how often we miss opportunities to experience God because we do not take time to engage in the little things. Instead, while looking to do big things for God, or trying to make our mark in the world, we overlook the fact that God meets us in events like rubbing feet, providing cold cups of water, making unannounced visits to prisoners or shut-ins, and giving a coat or blanket to someone who has none. In the economy of God's kingdom, it appears that little acts become big, and the big, ego-gratifying stuff is really insignificant.

If Jesus Were a Senior

When we read the Gospels, we sense that the people Jesus lifted up as role models were the ones who were faithful in *little things*. The widow who dropped a couple of pennies into the offering plate was praised for her generosity. The little boy who brought a few loaves of bread and a couple of fish for Jesus' use fed thousands. The person who went into the closet to pray, rather than praying in showy fashion before an enthralled public, was lifted up as an example of true piety. The woman who anointed Jesus' head with expensive perfume was heralded for the "beautiful thing" she did. In the Beatitudes Jesus reminded us that blessings come to those who are meek, poor in spirit, and full of mercy. Jesus presented a new model of success—a model that is very different from the "get-what-you-can-whatever-the-cost" attitude of the world. Jesus added another dimension to his model of success. In Matthew 25 he noted that what really mattered in the end was whether we fed the hungry, clothed the naked, and visited those who were in prison. Heroes, in Jesus' eyes, were—*and are*—those who embraced God's priorities for their lives.

Recently, one of my staff told me of a workshop she had attended. "The speaker pulled a participant from the audience," she began. "Then, unexpectedly, he started throwing small balls at the guy. You know, small bouncy balls about the size of an orange. Then the guy started mixing apples with the bouncy balls." At this point my staff worker started to laugh as she relived the moment. "It was really very funny. The poor guy was trying to catch the bouncy balls and apples as they were being tossed at him in rapid succession. Naturally the guy started dropping some of the balls and apples."

I could just picture this poor man on stage making a fool of himself. She continued, "Then shockingly the leader threw a glass cup at the guy. Of course, he couldn't catch it. Glass went everywhere as it smashed on the ground. Everyone went silent."

My staff worker shared the point of the exercise. The speaker was trying to convey that life is about making choices. The secret of life is learning how to juggle the different commitments and responsibilities that come our way. Some of these responsibilities are like the rubber balls—you can drop them and they bounce back. Some of life's responsibilities are like the apples. If you drop them they will bruise—and yes, it will hurt for a period of time when they're bruised—but ultimately it will be okay. However, some of our responsibilities are like the glass cup. If we drop it, it'll break and be useless. His point: make sure that your definition of success does not blind you to what are life's most important commitments and responsibilities. Whether we are in the corporate world, the social service sector, or the church community, it is easy—and probably inconsequential—to drop those things that are unimportant in life. But some things can break, cause damage to people, and are lost forever—things such as how we practice our faith, develop our relationships, and give attention to our family and the integrity with which we live our lives. They are the glass cups that must not be dropped.

Rabbi Shmuley Boteach reminds us of the cost of dropping *glass cups* in our lives when he writes,

> The Western world does not suffer much from poverty. But it does suffer from a lack of happy marriages and secure children. A man is labeled a success in our society if he is the chairman of a multinational corporation and has his own Gulfstream jet, even if he is on his fourth marriage and his children don't talk to him. The insecurities of one generation pass to the next. Loveless children are like deflated stock issues that never attracted the intention of investors. We grow up with an almost incurable feeling of insignificance, which leads to a manic devotion to professional success at any price.[41]

Rabbi Boteach vividly articulates the problem with "success" as it is defined by our culture. People can be applauded and upheld for their accomplishments, yet their families at the same time can be falling apart. For they have failed to do *the little things* well—like spending time with their children, strengthening their marriage, and loving the lowly.

Disciples of Jesus need to develop a clearly defined sense of biblical success before they begin to navigate their careers. If your idea of success is shaped primarily by the dominant culture, you will slowly find yourself chasing the illusion that satisfaction and inner peace can be found outside of God. As Augustine said, "Our hearts are restless until they rest in thee." True success, ultimately, is finding rest and contentment in God.

A Conversation with Jesus

It had been an interesting day on campus—an annual event called "Career Day," planned for juniors and seniors who are beginning to contemplate their futures. There were the high-tech companies promising IPOs and signing bonuses. There were large corporations offering well-compensated jobs with fast-track opportunities that would move one quickly up the corporate ladder. Special breakout lunch sessions were led by a diverse professional group of successful alumni. The event attracted droves of wide-eyed students looking for some fantastic career. There were promises of early retirement, job security, and abounding opportunities to get more.

After looking at every exhibit and talking forever, I arrived back to my dorm room emotionally exhausted and with a stack of brochures and business cards. I was overwhelmed.

There was a knock on my door.

"Who is it?" I yelled without opening the door. I really did not want to see anyone.

"It's I!" I knew the Voice by now and felt compelled to open the door.

"I thought you might want to talk. What'd you think about today?"

"I'm not sure," I responded, sounding somewhat perplexed. "I'm still processing all these promises of lucrative jobs and early retirement. Is that what life is all about?"

"It really comes down to," he began thoughtfully, "how you want to live your life. Just remember, money and good job security are fine, but they will not guarantee a fulfilling life. Behind the Armani suits and Rolexes there are a lot of empty, hurting people."

He was right. Outward appearances of success are no assurance that things are OK on the inside. I knew students on my dorm floor who came from prominent families that were esteemed in the community. Outwardly they had everything, but inwardly they had nothing. Those students were messed up.

"What then is a successful life?" I asked.

"Part of it is getting your priorities in the right place. There is a great line in the Bible that says to love God with all your heart, mind, strength, and soul; and love your neighbor as yourself. That's a pretty good starting place. Keep these priorities and you'll be pretty close."

"But that doesn't really answer my question," I added. "Sure, that sounds good, but does it really help when I am trying to decide what to do with my life?"

"I think you're asking the wrong question," replied my friend. "It's not so much what you end up doing with your life that is important— although I think you should use the gifts you've been given to bless the most people you possibly can—but how you go about your work."

"Oh."

"Do you always seek your own advancement? Do you love others, or just use them to get ahead? Are you humble? Do you cheat? Do you use your resources to bless others? Do you make others look better than yourself? Do you stand with those who have no voice? Do you spend time with your family and love your spouse?" He paused momentarily.

"Success is not so much what you do with your life, but how you live it." My Friend continued without giving me a chance to respond. "Do you

think I judge people according to what they do? Do I consider a doctor more worthy than a plumber? A lawyer more worthy than a teacher? A pastor more worthy than a salesperson? No. What matters is what they do with what they have been given. In the end you're going to be surprised. Some of the first will truly be last."

"Oh," again.

"I will leave you with this thought," said my Visitor. "Just remember that you belong to a different kingdom that has a different set of rules and a different standard for what is truly important. Mine is the kingdom in which you will find your true identity. And remember, unless you become like a little child, you can never find it."

I rubbed my eyes. My mind was working overtime. My Visitor was gone.

Remember:

What will you gain, if you own the whole world but destroy yourself?

Mark 8:36 CEV

Reflections for Students

1. In what ways does a biblical definition of success differ from our cultural definition of success? List these differences.

2. What can you begin to do now that might help you develop a definition of success that aligns itself with Jesus' definition of success?

3. Do you feel pressure to succeed in the eyes of your parents, your siblings, and your peer group? How do you deal with that pressure?

4. Is there someone you can identify who lives a life that embodies Jesus' definition of success? How does this person live life in a way that appeals to you?

5. What might you ask yourself, five years from now, that would help make sure your life is moving in the right direction?

For the Leader

Ask students in your group to do a survey with other students on campus—preferably students who are not active Christians. Ask them to answer the question, "What does a successful life look like for you?" Compile the definitions in a readable form.

Ask your fellowship group to come up with their definition of a successful life. Discuss the differences. Are there any?

Meditation

Lord,

Release me of the pressures I feel
   to be a success.
Fill my insecurities with
   your presence and peace,
so I will not be compelled to fill the void with things
   that are temporal—
   things that do not really matter.

Impart your wisdom so I can embrace
   your heart and your intentions for my life.
Teach me what it means
   to love well and be faithful in the little things.

Give me the faith to believe that
   your presence in the world advances through little acts
     of love,
   not mighty acts of power.

Amen

Chapter 7

Wardrobe Preparations:
Whom to Impress When We Dress

> We as a nation too often lack integrity, which might be
> described, in a loose and colloquial way, as the courage of
> one's convictions . . . too many of us nowadays neither
> mean what we say nor say what we mean. Moreover, we
> hardly expect anybody else to mean what they say either.
> Stephen L. Carter, *Integrity*

Heroes in Our Midst

Taxi! Taxi!

I jumped in. It was a short ride back to the airport and I just wanted to close my eyes and catch up on some much-needed sleep. Instead, on impulse, I said to the driver. "Where're you from?" The driver looked a little surprised by my interest.

"Mexico," he said flatly.

I glanced at his dashboard nametag and continued, "Sergio, what did you do in Mexico before you came to the States?"

"I used to work for the government." He paused. "I had an engineering degree and did a lot of stuff. Ya' know, dams, bridges, roads." His English was broken but understandable.

"Why'd you leave?" I asked, trying to understand how a government official with an engineering degree would end up in Seattle driving an airport shuttle for a car rental company.

"Corruption," he said with real feeling. "It's bad. It's really bad there." He glanced up at his rearview mirror. His eyes looked tired. They were eyes that knew pain. "It's a culture of corruption," he continued with some urgency. "Sure, every politician says they were going to clean up the jails and the schools. But it never changes. Hey, I reported sixteen guys . . .

guys who were working for the government. OK, so they were sent to jail. . . . But then they fired *me!*"

By this time any hint of my catching a nap had disappeared. I was captivated. "Was your life in danger?"

"Sure, three attempts were made on my life. I've got a hole in my leg from where they shot at me."

As the traffic crept along, we talked a little more about his situation, his family, and the difficulties of transitioning to a new country. Unfortunately we had then arrived at the airport.

Reluctantly, I collected my bags and shook his hand. I thanked this almost broken man for the ride. He vanished back into the van and sped off for his next pickup. I stared after the shuttle and then joined the swirl of busy travelers rushing to catch their planes.

As I sat on the plane and reflected on the sadly poignant conversation, I could not help but think of all the hurt and struggling people in the world—men and women who surely have tried to do the right thing and to lead honest and upright lives yet have been punished for their commitments and decisions.

Honesty and integrity apparently had cost my shuttle driver everything—his job, his status, and his country. For the sake of truth and honesty, Sergio, in the prime of his life, now drives an airport shuttle for eight dollars an hour—up and down, back and forth the same mile of strip malls and fast food joints, day after day.

I don't know whether Sergio was a man of faith. But what motivated him to swim against the tide of his culture and take such a heroic stand? Obviously Sergio knew the difference between right and wrong and had chosen the right.

Sergio will never know that he preached an important sermon to me that morning, not one of words but a sermon from his life. God's Spirit decided that I needed to hear a message about integrity and Sergio became God's messenger.

Sergio embodied the challenge of Dr. Martin Luther King Jr. when he claimed from a cell in a Birmingham jail, "We will have to repent in this generation not merely for the hateful words and actions of the bad people, but for the appalling silence of the good people."[42] Sergio embodied what so few people today seem to value—honesty and integrity and a willingness to pay the price for what he believed to be true. They will probably never make a movie about Sergio, nor will he grace the cover of *Time* magazine as the "Person of the Year."

But Sergio, common everyday citizen, did hold back the darkness for a brief period of time. Sergio, common everyday citizen, still has his soul. And who knows what God can do when a seed of truth is planted in a field of lies and deception?

The Worst Sermon I Ever Preached

I remember the worst sermon I ever preached. Usually public speakers have a pretty good idea that they have struck out when no one approaches them after the talk. The crowd just walks past without looking you in the eye or saying hello. Perhaps I'm just a little sensitive—shouldn't let my ego get in the way—and should trust that God is not dependent on my ability to reach the hearts of people.

But I was bad.

To make it worse, it was Easter Sunday—an outdoor sunrise service at 6:00 A.M. Because the service was early and outdoors, I already had two strikes against me before I even opened my mouth. (One needs a jolt of resurrection power to stir a crowd before the sun comes up.)

It was also a family service. You know, kids in diapers, toddlers, moms, dads, grandparents—all hungry—on their way to an all-you-can-eat buffet breakfast bar. Does it sound like I'm making excuses? Three strikes.

Since I had no idea how to communicate the resurrection of Jesus to a screaming two-year-old, I decided to try another approach. Rather than focusing on the historical reality of the resurrection, I picked a wonderful text from Colossians 3, paraphrased by Eugene Peterson in *The Message*. The apostle vividly wrote and Peterson colorfully translated,

> Don't lie to one another. You're done with that old life. It's like a filthy set of ill-fitting clothes you've stripped off and put in the fire. Now you're dressed in a new wardrobe. Every item of your new way of life is custom-made by the Creator, with his label on it. All the old fashions are now obsolete. Words like Jewish and non-Jewish, religious and irreligious, insider and outsider, uncivilized and uncouth, slave and free, mean nothing. From now on everyone is defined by Christ, everyone is included in Christ.
>
> So, chosen by God for this new life of love, dress in the wardrobe God picked out for you: compassion, kindness, humility, quiet strength, discipline. Be even-tempered, content with second place, quick to forgive an offense. Forgive as quickly and completely as the Master forgave

you. And regardless of what else you put on, wear love. It's
your basic, all-purpose garment. Never be without it.
                                        Colossians 3:9–14[43]

The image Paul presented to his audience is powerful.
Everybody can relate to clothing—especially clothes that we
have outgrown. Paul reminded the people that the resurrection
of Jesus made them *new creatures;* that meant they should be
wearing a *new wardrobe.* To illustrate the point for my audience
I decided (yes, here's where it began to go awry) to wear under
my regular suit jacket an old sports jacket I had worn in high
school. The plan was to take off the new suit jacket part way
through the sermon and expose my *old clothing,* which was obviously too tight and too small. The sleeves came halfway up my
arms and, with a checkered design and lapels the size of New
Jersey, the coat was obviously twenty years out of style.

At that point in the sermon I was going to talk about how
some of us are still wearing the same "clothing" we wore twenty
years ago. I wanted to connect my too-clever little sermon illustration to the reality that well-intended church folk spend hundreds of dollars each year on purchasing new suits, dresses, and
bonnets for Easter Sunday. And then they fail to put on the real
clothing of the resurrection—the "custom-made garment" of
our Creator. That garment includes our willingness to move
beyond labeling people, a willingness to embrace people who
are different from us, and the desire to be compassionate, kind,
patient, humble, and loving people. That was the kind of clothing Paul wants us to wear Easter Sunday.

Unfortunately, when the moment came to walk down from
the podium and take off the sports jacket, I could not get the
microphone to release from its mount. I had to make a quick
decision. Without a microphone, the four hundred people
would not be able to hear my point. If I stayed behind the pulpit, they would not be able to really see the contrast in clothing.
It was the perfect no-win situation. I decided to forgo the visual
aspect of the sermon and not take off my suit jacket.

Instead, I stayed behind the pulpit and tried to reconstruct
the remaining part of the sermon. By that time I was too flus-
tered and never really pulled myself back on track. Instead of
gaining energy and moving toward a climax, the sermon fiz-
zled. I was sure people sensed my struggle and wondered why
my old checkered blazer kept peeking through the opening in
my suit.

Fortunately, the power and truth of Scripture do not depend on one's ability to communicate. As I later threw my sermon notes into my filing cabinet, I was comforted to remember that Paul's metaphor of new clothing still jumps off the pages of the Bible and challenges us with *how* to live in the workplace. As God's people we are called to wear clothing that often conflicts with the clothing the world tells us to wear. Our Armani designer suits and Italian leather shoes may impress our potential employer that we can "dress for success" and can make good first impressions. But underneath the wool and shiny leather, something needs to tell who we really are in Christ—people who have different motives and a different set of priorities.

Dwelling on Paul's New Clothing

Fortunately, over the years I have learned many valuable lessons from my mistakes. Often, however, the lessons have been painful.

I once hired an individual for a position within our ministry. Confident and handsomely dressed, he was great in his interviews and had an impressive resume, a great smile, and a firm handshake. Since I was hiring the individual to interact with our corporate supporters, I thought that these qualities would be essential, especially since most of our staff had no desire to put on a suit and a tie and meet the CEOs of supporting companies. So I really believed that this young man would represent the ministry well to the outside world. With the approval of my staff, I hired him.

Within two weeks it became apparent that I had made a huge mistake. The young man's self-confidence was really arrogance. His ability to dress well was just a cover-up for his neurotic behavior. And his smile was a mask—it did not reflect any inner joy. He turned out to be a slick salesman whom people did not trust. He turned people off to the ministry—including our supporters. I fired him before he did too much damage. I learned from the experience that people—even high-powered corporate types—would rather give money and support to people with integrity, even if they wore blue jeans and sweatshirts. People are wary of those well-dressed persons they sense lack integrity. All of us want authenticity. People want to see integrity in those with whom they relate. Integrity is more important than the kind of clothing people wear. Fancy suits may make good first impressions, but in the long run honest, hard-working people will keep their jobs and be a tremendous asset to those with whom they work.

Paul's challenge to the church community of Colossae was that the clothing one wears is critical. But Christians wear a new kind of clothing, given by the Spirit of God. It is the kind of clothing that moves one away from the characteristics of our former selves and replaces those self-centered characteristics with attributes that reveal the heart of God.

Integrity

If there is one overarching theme in the third chapter of Colossians, it is *integrity*. Paul challenged then and challenges now all those who have embraced the good news of the Gospel: Live your life in a way that is consistent with the teachings of Jesus. Paul rebukes those who try to live a double life. He reminds us that our old lives—lives filled with evil desires, lust, ruthless greed, malice, slander, gossip, and lying—should be "put to death." It is critical for Paul that Christians become people whose doctrine and lifestyle coincide. After all, that *is* the definition of integrity. Integrity means *whole*. Integrity means there is a consistency between what we say and what we do. Paul nudges the people of Colossae, and us, toward the place where our faith and lifestyle are seamlessly woven together.

I believe that integrity is one of the most challenging aspects of being Christian. It is easy to stand in front of people and share the teachings of Christ, and yet it is difficult to put those same teachings into practice. It is easy to go to church on Sunday, and yet it is difficult to carry our worship and faith into the workplace during the week. Many people live an impressive public religious life but then live a very different private life. Integrating the teachings of our faith into our daily lifestyle is the true test. That is why Paul claims in verse 17 of the same chapter, "Let every detail in your lives—words, actions, whatever—be done in the name of the Master, Jesus, thanking God the Father every step of the way."[44] When we allow everything in our lives to be done in the name of Jesus, we live a life of integrity.

Role Models of Integrity

When my wife and I first decided to buy a house, we needed some help with the down payment. We could not quite scrape together enough money for the bank to give us the loan. Fortunately my father was able to help with the down payment. He did not just give us the money. There was a contingency, a subclause: "When you can pay the loan back, pay it back." There were no contracts, no dates, and no interest to be paid. When we got ahead financially, he wanted us to repay him.

Then came a surprise. When we went to sign the papers for the bank, they asked if we had been given any money from other sources. If so, we needed the person to sign a waiver stating that the money was a gift and not a loan. "Send it to your dad," said my wife, Pamela. "He'll sign it."

"No, I don't think he will," I replied.

"Wha'da'ya' mean?" retorted Pam. "It's not like it's a real loan."

"You don't know my dad," I continued. "I guarantee you he will not sign it."

"I'll bet you," challenged Pam. She really was in love with that house. "I'll bet you a week of wonderfully cooked dinners and cleanup afterwards."

"You don't know what you're doing," I reassured my naive wife. "You're going to lose the bet."

That night we called my father. We explained the situation and asked him if he would sign the document. "No, I *cannot* consent to signing the form. To sign would be dishonest. I can't lie."

Pam was blown away by my father's response. Actually, what really surprised her was my knowledge of my father's response even before I asked him for the favor. For after watching him live his life and faith in my presence for more than twenty years, I knew that he would not sign something that caused him to sacrifice his integrity. Integrity is central to my father's life. He was raised in a generation when a handshake and a person's word were better than a legal contract. Now the world is a very different place. A person's word often is worth little. Promises are broken. Lying is accepted behavior—regardless of a person's role in society. "You are only a liar if a court determines you are one." "Nobody expects people to tell the truth." Too often even employers expect their employees to do whatever it takes to deceive the public and help the bottom line. Maintaining one's integrity is a difficult challenge in this world.

But people of integrity are a tremendous gift to their children, their colleagues, their church, and their community. They are a living testimony that a life of integrity *can* be lived in our world. The heroes are a gift because they model courage at tremendous personal cost, like being overlooked for a job promotion, losing an important contract, or having to quit a position because of the pressure to compromise. Maintaining integrity can be a costly enterprise. For Paul nothing was more important than a consistency between what we preach and how we act.

Stories of Integrity

Great literature can provide models of integrity when we begin to feel discouraged. One character that challenges me is the slave Tom in Harriet Beecher Stowe's classic, *Uncle Tom's Cabin.* Tom is portrayed as a man of tremendous personal courage who will not compromise what he knows to be true. Although clad in pauper's clothes, Tom wears the kinds of clothing—kindness, humility, quiet strength—that Paul talks of in Colossians.

In the book Stowe records a moving and powerful account of personal integrity. In one scene, Tom stands up to his master, Simon Legree, and comes out the undisputed moral victor. Legree, the slave owner, has decided that a particular slave woman, after a long day of picking cotton, needs a severe beating. According to Legree, she has not met her quota of cotton for the day. He calls Tom over to do the dirty task.

"And now," said Legree, "come, here, you Tom. You see, I tell ye I didn't buy ye jest for the common work; I mean to promote ye, and make a driver of ye; and tonight ye may jest as well begin to get yer hand in. Now, ye jest take this here gal and flog her; ye've seen enough on't to know how."

"I beg mas'r's pardon," said Tom; "hopes mas'r won't set me at that. It's what I ain't used to—never did—and can't do, no way possible."

"Ye'll larn a pretty smart chance of things ye never did know, before I've done with ye!" said Legree, taking up a cow-hide, and striking Tom a heavy blow across the cheek, and following up the infliction by a shower of blows.

"There!" he said, as he stopped to rest; "now, will ye tell me ye can't do it?"

"Yes, mas'r," said Tom, putting up his hand, to wipe the blood, that trickled down his face. "I'm willing to work, night and day, and work while there's life and breath in me; but this yer thing I can't feel it right to do—and, mas'r, I never shall do it—*never!*"

"Legree looked stupefied and confounded; but at last burst forth:

"What! Ye blasted black beast! Tell me ye don't think it *right* to do what I tell ye! What have any of you cussed cattle to do with thinking what's right? I'll put a stop to it! Why, what do ye think ye are? Maybe ye think ye'r a gentleman, master Tom, to be a telling your master what's right, and what ain't! So you pretend it's wrong to flog the gal!"

"I think so, mas'r," said Tom; "the poor creature's sick and feeble; 't would be downright cruel, and it's what I never will do, nor begin to. Mas'r, if you mean to kill me, kill me; but, as to my raising my hand agin any one here, I never shall—I'll die first!"

Tom spoke in a mild voice, but with a decision that could not be mistaken. Legree shook with anger; his greenish eyes glared fiercely, and his very whiskers seemed to curl with passion; but, like some ferocious beast, that plays with its victim before he devours it he kept back his strong impulse to proceed to immediate violence, and broke out into bitter raillery.

"Well, here's a pious dog, at last, let down among us sinners! A saint, a gentleman, and no less, to talk to us sinners about our sins! Powerful hold critter, he must be! Here, you rascal, you make believe to be so pious—didn't you never hear, out of yer Bible, 'Servants, obey yer masters'? Didn't I pay down twelve hundred dollars cash, for all there is inside yer old cussed black shell? Ain't yer mine, now, body and soul?" he said, giving Tom a violent kick with his heavy boot; "tell me!"

In the very depth of physical suffering, bowed by brutal oppression, this question shot a gleam of joy and triumph through Tom's soul. He suddenly stretched himself up, and, looking earnestly to heaven, while the tears and blood that flowed down his face mingled, he exclaimed:

"No! No! no! my soul ain't yours, mas'r! You haven't bought it—ye can't buy it! It's been bought and paid for, by one that is able to keep it—no matter, no matter, you can't harm me!"

"I can't," said Legree with a sneer; "we'll see—we'll see! Here, Sambo, Quimbo, give this dog such a breakin' in as he won't get over, this month!"[45]

Integrity. Courage. Instead of compromising and capitulating to the pressures of being cruel to another human being, Tom remains committed to what he knows God wants of him—to be loving, kind, and compassionate toward another human being, especially a human who is weak and feeble. Because of these convictions, Tom takes a stand against his master regardless of the personal cost. Even though Tom has no power and is treated as nothing but an animal on the social ladder, he demonstrates his moral superiority by maintaining his integrity. Tom is a new creature. Despite being stripped of his clothing and bloodied, Tom wears the clothing of the resurrection. Tom is so rooted in his faith, so convinced that Jesus 'owns' his soul, and so courageous to live out these convictions that he is willing to endure the brutality Simon Legree can do to his body.

Tom certainly is an example and inspiration for those of us who long to live lives that reflect the Creator's wardrobe. Daily, we need to strip off the clothing of our self-centered nature and put on the clothing of God's new creation. As we align our faith convictions with our daily practice, we will truly become God's people.

Fill the Wardrobe: Compassion, Kindness, Humility, and Quiet Strength

Paul spells out in Colossians 3 the quality of clothing we disciples are supposed to wear. Besides living a life of integrity, followers of Jesus are explicitly told to wear compassion, kindness, humility, quiet strength, and discipline. Again, these kinds of clothing often contradict the clothing that the world calls us to wear. If we want to be successful in our careers, surely we cannot be kind and humble and willing to settle for second place. This is not the American way. But the way of Jesus is not the American way. Jesus calls us to a new way.

Even with that straightforward admonition, it is hard to spell out exactly what it means to put on the kinds of clothes Paul commands. We can look up what the New Testament words mean in the Greek and try to discern their meanings from various commentaries, but even if we intellectually understand what Paul was saying to his audience, do we know how to translate these words into action? Do we know how to make this knowledge real? Sometimes I find that the best way to make sense of Scripture in daily life is to see it lived out in the life of another person. When we see it lived out before us in the life of a brother or sister, we can say, "*That's* how I am supposed to live."

Examples in My Midst

A few months ago I caught a glimpse of what it meant to wear compassion, kindness, humility, and quiet strength. I saw it in the life of one of my former students.

It had been a long, tiring week, full of financial pressures, staff conflicts, and bothersome details. My idealistic vision of a significant ministry had gotten lost in the fatigue of minutia. I was more than ready to go home for the weekend.

"Natasia Burgess is here to see you, Bruce," phoned my receptionist.

"Have her come in," I responded unthinkingly as I glanced at my calendar. There was nothing scheduled for three o'clock. Had I forgotten to write the appointment down? "Natasia Burgess," I muttered to myself. "Natasia Burgess?" I sifted through my memory of faces and names. Nothing.

I was glad when I recognized her immediately as she walked in. "I haven't seen you in years," I said heartily and a bit relieved. "Can it have been your high school graduation? You've hardly changed a bit. Is your hair shorter?" Her facial expressions had matured, but she still had that great smile. She looked great. "Have a seat," I said, genuinely glad to see her.

We began to catch up on the last five years of her life. With pride and a sly smile Natasia said that she was going to graduate from nursing school in three months. It had been a long, rough road, though. Many times she had had to quit school to work and save money for her next tuition. "But I hung in there—took night classes, worked part-time, did whatever I had to to make it through. And then I adopted a child."

Bang. That was it, not embroidered, just "I adopted a child." I meet a lot of teen mothers, but not often do I meet twenty-three-year-old single women voluntarily adopting a baby.

"Sionna's two. I've had her since she was six months old," she continued with a smile.

"Wow. You adopted a baby?" I said, trying to get my thoughts around the idea of this young woman struggling to work and keep herself in school while obviously adding real complications to her young life.

"It was my cousin Brea's baby," she began. "I went by her house one night to visit. She wasn't home. But I went in and found the baby just lying on the floor. No crib. No diaper. All she had on was a T-shirt wrapped around her legs. I discovered that the poor child was drinking *evaporated milk*! Can you imagine that? A mother leaving her child to feed herself evaporated milk?"

"That's terrible, Natasia. What'd you do?"

"Well, what could I do? I took the baby home! The next day I contacted my cousin and told her that I had the baby and that I would watch her until she got her life back together. I've had the baby ever since."

"But why'd you do that, Natasia? My goodness, you're in the prime of your life, and that's tough enough without adding a child's care on top of all your other challenges. How come?"

Natasia smiled. "God." That was it. "God's the reason I took the child." She didn't expand on her explanation, and I sensed I wouldn't hear anything more. Her statement said it all.

But let me tell you that as a father of three children, I know some of the struggles associated with raising children, going to school, and holding a full-time job. But I have the advantage of a full-time marriage partner, a solid income, and my college years well behind me. Natasia has none of those things. I said with admiration, "How do you ever do it all?"

"I'm not sure, 'cause sometimes it's difficult when I get *really* tired. I come home from school and work and know I have to study, but then I prefer to spend some time playing with the baby. She needs that attention. So I feed her, get her ready for bed, and make her lunch for the next day. *Then* I try to hit the books. But sometimes I don't have any energy left and just fall asleep at the kitchen table."

As I listened to the young woman who was three months away from graduation—a major accomplishment in her life—I was reminded that there are unsung heroes in our midst. Embodied before me was a living Good Samaritan, a young woman moved by compassion and kindness, who responded to a baby's desperate need. Without any accolades or fanfare she assumed the financial and emotional responsibilities attached to raising a child. Like the Good Samaritan, whom Jesus cites as an example of loving our neighbor, Natasia is a living sermon of unselfish, costly love.

Most college seniors I know would never entertain the idea of taking on the responsibility of raising a child—certainly not the child of a cousin. Rather, they would spend their free time dating, hanging out, or partying away their last days on campus. They would be so focused on increasing their GPA that they could never consider sacrificing precious study time to change diapers and arrange for day care. I told her how proud I was of her.

We chatted on a bit more about old times, and then she had to leave. At the door she turned and said, "Ya know, Bruce, when Sionna gets a little older, I'll bring her around. I want her to be exposed to the same love I received when I used to be involved in the ministry here."

That was it. The one who had experienced love and kindness was now the one giving the love and kindness. Natasia had seen the clothing of the Creator worn by former staff workers and counselors—people who showed her compassion, kindness, and love. When it was her turn, she demonstrated the same.

And that's how it *should* be.

If Jesus Were a Senior

The year 2002 was full of corporate scandals. Enron, one of the largest companies in the nation, collapsed almost overnight. A reputable accounting firm had allegedly been doctoring the books. Once viewed as an example of everything that was good about capitalism, Enron quickly became an American tragedy, robbing thousands of employees of their jobs, their pensions, and their savings. What seemed invincible and secure one moment was gone the next. The country was shocked. As the stories of the internal politics surfaced in *Time* and *Newsweek* magazines, one quickly realized that a number of ego-driven, selfish, power-hungry people created a culture of greed. That culture of greed led to a culture of dishonestly that ultimately led to the collapse of the company. The corporate directors wore the clothing of deception, power, arrogance, and success at all costs.

One does not have to be an elitist manager of a megacorporation to get caught up in the seduction of money, power, and corruption. Each day Christians are faced with decisions that either reflect the values of God's heart or reflect the values of the world's desires.

A good friend who owns a construction company told me that it is hard to survive in his business without being intentionally malicious. "It's hard for me to love those who intentionally stab me in the back." Yet he refuses to play to game, and after thirty years he is still in the business. He has not lost his soul. He is respected and profitable. He has tried to wear *the clothing of the resurrection*.

Another friend is about to graduate from medical school. "It is hard to keep my faith in this culture that makes science the ultimate god." The competition is intense. The temptation to succeed at all costs is tremendous. And yet she has decided to try to wear the clothing of compassion and humility.

Another friend recently quit his six-figure job because the company was asking him to lie. "I just couldn't do it and sleep at night." He had put his family at risk, but he had decided that integrity is more important than a paycheck.

It is critical for students to begin the process of selecting their wardrobes before they get too far into their careers and vocations. Life is a series of choices. These choices will lead us either closer to the heart of God or farther from God's intentions for our lives. If we clothe ourselves in the clothing of righteousness, we will find that our careers and vocations will bring life and love into both our life and those lives that we touch. Check out your wardrobe.

A Conversation with Jesus

"You look good!" Startled, I turned around. Combing my hair and dressing is usually a private event. I am not used to having Someone watch me.

"Thanks," I added as I finished tying my shoes. I was feeling pretty good in my khakis and blue oxford, button-down shirt. Usually I dress in sweatshirts and blue jeans, but today I was presenting my senior thesis.

"Have you put on my *wardrobe today?" continued my Visitor. I was caught a little off guard. Finding clean clothes was a big enough challenge. I had no idea what my Guest meant by "my wardrobe."*

"What you are talking about?"

"Let's just say you should worry less about what you put on the outside and more about what goes on the inside. Sure, it's great to look good, but don't put too much stock in the kind of clothes you wear or the kind of shoes you put on. People know pretense." He went on to explain. "You're going to go out into the work world soon." I did not need to be reminded. Graduation was just around the corner. I had yet to find a job. I had no idea what I was going to do with my major. The anxiety was beginning to set in. No job. No place to live.

"You're going to be confronted with decisions everyday, and I am concerned about the kinds of decisions you will make. Anybody can wear sharp-looking clothes and climb the success ladder. But I care about what is underneath it all—what will actually guide your decisions?"

My Guest did not stop. "When you arrived in college, you were wearing one set of clothing. You were still working through some of that "earthly nature" stuff—anger, selfish ambition, and greed. Those are not the clothes I want you to wear at the workplace. Those old habits will surface soon enough. Be prepared."

For a moment I thought about his words. I had changed a lot in the past four years. I came into college with the ambition of getting a good education so I could get a good job and acquire all kinds of wonderful things. But things had changed. Those were not my priorities now. I was thinking differently. Now I was thinking that it was more important who I became, as opposed to what I became. Hey, I had really started to build a new kind of wardrobe.

"Be prepared. Yes, yes, I'll remember," I mumbled as I sped out the door.

Remember:

The world is waiting for new saints, ecstatic men and women who are so deeply rooted in the love of God that they are free to imagine a new international order. Most people cling to old ways and prefer the security of their misery to the insecurity of their joy. But the few who dare to sing the new song of peace are the new St. Francises of our time, offering a glimpse of the new order that is being born out of the ruin of the old.

Henri Nouwen

Reflections for Students

1. What was a favorite piece of clothing you wore in high school? Why did you like it so much? Have you discarded it? Why or why not?

2. What pressures and challenges do you think you will face when you enter the work world? What are you doing to prepare yourself for these pressures?

3. What does integrity mean to you? Name somebody who embodies integrity. Why do you see this person as someone of integrity?

4. Is taking a stand for something you believe in difficult for you? What consequences have you experienced because of your beliefs and commitments?

For the Leader

Find a variety of professional people, representing different vocations, who integrate their faith into all aspects of their daily lives. Have your students prepare questions for these guests. The questions should really delve into the tough issues that a person faces in the workplace. Find people who will be honest with their struggles and attempts to live faithfully for God.

Meditation

Lord,

Thanks for the promise of a new wardrobe.
Thanks that I do not have to be a slave to the latest styles and
    fashions.
Thanks that I can let go of some of these old garments that I
    have worn for too long.

I ask for the clothing of compassion,
    so that I can respond to those who hurt.
I ask for the clothing of kindness,
    so that I can bless others.
I ask for the clothing of humility,
    so that I can put others before myself.
I ask for the clothing of quiet strength,
    so that I can persevere despite difficulties.
I ask for the clothing of love,
    so that I can display your nature to the world.

Amen

Chapter 8

Community Preparations:
Why We Need Others

In and through community lies the salvation of the world.
Nothing is more important.
Yet it is virtually impossible to describe community meaningfully
to someone who has never experienced it—
and most of us have never had an experience of true community.
M. Scott Peck, The Different Drum

Let him [or her] who cannot be alone beware of community.
Let him who is not in community beware of being alone.
Dietrich Bonhoeffer, Life Together

Community Works

"Bob is thinking about leaving our community." The staff workers surrounded me for this unscheduled meeting. They had heard that Bob was contemplating leaving our inner-city work, and no one in the group wanted to see him move on.

"It would be helpful for each of us to share what Bob's departure might mean to the ministry and to each of us personally," I continued. Bob was a real asset to our community, a wonderful musician and worship leader, creative, great with kids, personable, and deeply spiritual. People liked him.

"Where are you going, Bob?" asked one staff member. "What's your plan?"

"I'm not sure yet, perhaps back to school. I'm thinking about a career in music—you know, maybe do some recordings." We all knew that this was not pie-in-the-sky dreaming. Bob was a very talented song writer. He had written numerous worship songs and songs for kids. Bob could make a living in the recording industry.

"How will you support yourself?" came another voice of concern.

"I'm not sure. I'll probably get a day job and then write music at night."

"Are you sure that you can do all that?" questioned another. "You need energy to compose good music. I tried working full-time while going to school. It's tough with rent, utilities, and other expenses. Before you know it, you're not writing. You're just exhausted at the end of the day."

These were real questions and ideas that Bob had not yet considered. His coworkers didn't speak in an authoritarian way, rather as peers who were concerned about his future and the future life of their community. Bob listened intently. "Bob, have you ever thought that you could fulfill some of your goals right here?" asked his roommate. "We could change your schedule a little and give you more time to write. We could even help raise some money needed for a recording." His roommate looked at me for approval. I nodded in agreement.

"Yeah!" chimed in another. "We need you, Bob. We need a musician. Without your music, my work with the kids will be diminished. Your music keeps me going."

The others all shared encouraging accounts of how Bob's songs had enriched their ministries. "Anyway, our little community just *needs* a song writer—somebody who captures our experience through song." The community was affirming Bob's role as that person. Bob's confident smile was back. God's calling for his life was becoming clear.

By the end of the meeting Bob had decided: he was going to recommit himself to our work. The staff talked about how we could juggle our schedules and responsibilities so that Bob would have more time to compose. Staff voluntarily picked up Bob's commitments, sacrificially taking on more duties, so their gifted brother could fulfill his calling and use his gifts more fully as a song writer and worship leader.

Over the next few years, Bob wrote thoughtful and creative new worship choruses. We were blessed every time we gathered for worship and prayer. He wrote songs about the struggles of families and children growing up in the inner city. He captured the feelings and struggles of our team and put them into words. He became our musical voice.

What would have happened if Bob had left our community when he first thought about it? We would have been deprived of a very essential ingredient. But when Bob shared his thoughts, something special happened, both in Bob's life and in the lives of all who were present.

When Bob was affirmed and given space to grow and blossom, the others in the community learned that each person has an important role to play in helping others discover their spiritual gifts and talents. That day the community learned about *community*.

Why Community?

Christian *community* is one of God's great gifts for those who seek to live out their faith with vitality. It is in community that we see ourselves more clearly. In community we discern God's calling and find the ongoing encouragement to persevere in the midst of obstacles. Connecting with a healthy community can be the most important decision we make after we finish college.

But where do we find such a *community*? Is it by moving to some small Midwestern town? Do we find community in the church we join? Will it be an organization or a country club? The question of where we find a community is critical.

However, before we start looking for community, we need to develop a working definition of a community—the type of community that actually can help a person grow in faith and find his or her calling. For the truth is, a person can go to a church and never experience community. People can live in a small town all their lives yet feel extremely isolated and never experience intimacy. People may join country clubs and civic groups yet never move beyond superficial engagement with other people. Community is not a place or just any group of people. *Community* is about the quality of relationships, values, and mission that a group shares.

M. Scott Peck defines community as "a group of individuals who have learned how to communicate honestly with each other, whose relationships go deeper than their masks of composure, and who have developed some significant commitment to 'rejoice together, mourn together,' and to 'delight in each other, make others' conditions our own.'"[46] For Peck, true community has a much deeper dimension than simply attending a religious service or playing poker with a group of friends once a week. Community, according to Peck, is about people truly *knowing* each other.

Sadly, it can be hard to find *community*. In our fast-paced, aggressive, ruggedly individualistic culture, true community is rare. I remember talking to a sixty-year-old man who began to share how he had recently joined a small Bible study and prayer group. It was the first time in his life that he had met with such a group of people on a regular basis. *The fellowship changed his life.* "I've been going to church for forty years, but I have never had friends with whom I could share my struggles and prayers. This is the best thing that has ever happened to me." As I listened to the man's comments, I was delighted but disheartened that it had taken him forty years to find a place where he could be vulnerable and find others who were deeply interested in his life. He had gone to church for years, but he had never found a *community.*

George Barna illustrates this deficiency of community in our culture in an article titled "The Church of Tomorrow," where he highlights the fact that the church is not meeting the empty void that so many people in our culture experience. "Several hundred thousand adults are already totally dependent upon the Internet for the entire content of their spiritual experience. Millions more will join them, giving up on congregations, campuses and Sunday Schools to find some spiritual connection through their computer."[47] Barna goes on to conclude, "How is this possible? Because for many, perhaps even most of these cyber-congregants, *faith is about community.* They are striving to develop long-term, intense, honest, productive relationships with others who are on the same spiritual journey, searching for similar outcomes: relationships, self-knowledge, interaction with God."[48] What Barna so powerfully expresses is that people *are* looking for community, for honest relationships—a place where they can struggle with their faith and their sense of calling. If they cannot find it in a church, they will turn to the Internet, to a bar, to a social club.

One of reasons, I believe, students lose their passion for God after college is because they never find a community that really supports them in their faith journey. Finding and participating in a vibrant Christian community *after* college is critical. Community can provide accountability, teach vital people skills, help us clarify our calling, and be the source of encouragement when life gets overwhelming or we become discouraged.

Accountability

After finishing college, I had hoped that I would become more spiritually disciplined. For some reason I thought that discipline would get easier as the years rolled on. I was wrong. As a matter of fact, I still struggle. I struggle with getting up in the morning and spending quality time with Jesus. Even when I do manage to pull myself out of bed, I have been known to nod off a time or two . . . or three. . . . My study of Scripture can be erratic. Perhaps some Christians find discipline easy—I know some who can jump out of bed every morning at 5:30 A.M. and spend an hour and a half in prayer and solitude. But these people are the exception. And that's not me.

Each year I ask our college volunteers, during the first week of January, what they want to improve in their lives during the coming year. Inevitably they respond, "I want to spend more *quality* time with God." Six months later, when I ask how they are doing, the response is usually, "I want to spend more *quality* time with God." Most people struggle to grow in their faith without the presence, encouragement, and accountability of other believers. So for the past fifteen years, I have met every Monday morning for prayer, worship, and devotional study with a group of Christians who desire to put their faith into practice. I realize this practice is not the norm for most people in the workplace or graduate school. Consequently, I feel blessed that my work affords me this kind of experience each week.

But I want to be honest. Many times our worship experience is inspiring and creative. Other times our worship is dry and boring. Sometimes the devotional time is insightful and thought-provoking; other times it is tedious. Sometimes the prayer time is intense and emotional; other times it is routine. But regardless of the emotional quality of this scheduled community gathering, I have found it critical for myself and those with whom I work. Sure, at times our staff staggers into the sanctuary at 8:00 A.M. with eyes half open, not feeling particularly spiritual—or much else. But, regardless of how each of us feels at the time, we have all agreed that we need the accountability of gathering together. Left to our own devices, we would find it easy to neglect beginning each week reconnecting with one another and with God.

Our community is vital for each member of our ministry team. Weekly we are reminded that we are not simply social workers, camp counselors, administrators, or fundraisers. This event reminds us that we are all ministers—regardless of the tasks we perform—and we do not labor alone. Through the testimonies of other community members we find strength, learn new things about God, and renew our commitment to service.

Our community also has built in other gatherings during the week that pull us back to the Source of our vision and mission. On Wednesday mornings ministry *leaders* pray and share together, communicating concerns, struggles, joys, and sorrows, how we see God at work in our individual ministries and in our personal lives. We use the time to support one another and pray for others in our community. It is an important time for each of us, as we transcend the formalities of professional relationships and create a place where we can grow in our faith.

So find or develop a community that has *regularly* scheduled opportunities to come together for worship, study, and sharing. It will be absolutely vital for your personal growth and ongoing commitment to discipleship. You need this kind of accountability. I need this kind of accountability. We all need this kind of accountability.

The Urgent Need for People Skills

Every summer our organization recruits fifty to seventy college students. Students come from all over the world to spend a summer in the inner city. They discover that it is an intense experience. The food is basic, the living conditions are rugged, and the students live in close relationship with one another. Initially, most students are sure that their greatest challenges will be faced on the tough streets of Camden, that their greatest struggles will be with difficult children, rebellious teenagers, or cultural differences. Little do they realize that the greatest challenge they face will come from the other students with whom they live. Other students with whom they share a bathroom and kitchen will cause most of their stress, frustration, anger, and sadness.

When they arrive, they don't know that it is in the living together that they will learn their most important life lessons. They will learn *how to confront* and *how to be confronted*. Through these exchanges one of life's most critical tools will be developed. They will learn important lessons about themselves and about how to deal with other people. Through truthful confrontation, unique opportunities for personal growth are created.

Here's a brief picture of what it's like. Ten college volunteers are living together for the summer in the inner city. They live in a big three-story house. The men live on the third floor. The women live on the second. The students come from diverse Christian backgrounds—Baptists, Lutherans, Catholics, and an assortment of other denominations. They are doing ministry together—running day camps, mentoring teens, and doing outreach programs.

One day Gwen, a twenty-two-year-old senior from a western university, was washing dishes in the kitchen. She'd had a long, hot day of work. Gwen was a real servant, worked hard and had had a great day at camp. Her art class had gone exceptionally well. She was feeling good about her summer.

In came Brian as the kitchen screen door slammed. He'd been on the basketball court all afternoon. Brian was from a small liberal arts college in Idaho, though he lived at home. It was his first mission experience and his first time away from his parents. He was really thrilled that he could use his basketball skills to reach kids. The handsome, rough-edged, engaging young man had had two great hours on the court coaching his junior high kids. "Great to see ya in the kitchen, Gwen. It's where women belong," chuckled Brian, who then chugged a quart of orange juice. "I just love this Christian community stuff. Everybody serving one another." He paused for a few seconds. "Gwen, those brownies you girls made last night were really delicious. Do you think you could whip up some more while I take a nap? I'm going to take a shower, then catch a few Z's."

Brian had led a very pampered life with a domineering mother. He had a good heart but had no clue as to the effect of his comments. He just needed to be educated and lovingly confronted. Just then Michelle and Lori walked in. "Hey, Gwen, everything all right? You look a little bothered and annoyed."

Gwen exploded: "That Brian! I thought he was a decent guy. Turns out he's a dinosaur—a real chauvinist pig. He told me *women belong in the kitchen*! Can you believe it? And then he had the nerve to tell me to *whip up some brownies* while he takes a nap!"

"I don't believe it!" responded Michelle, believing all of it. "Well, I've lost any respect for him. Wait'll I tell the others."

"Yeah, I agree," confirmed Lori. *"Who does he think he is?"*

Unfortunately, I have seen the scenario played out numerous times as new missioners arrive. Brian had no sense of what he had done and never got confronted. Consequently, he never learned or had the opportunity to grow from his ignorance. Rather than following a biblical directive, Gwen chose to do what most of us continually do—gossip or deal with the problem indirectly.

I believe that this style of dealing with one another is one of the great faults of the Christian community. *Christian brothers and sisters do not know how to confront one another.* We would rather avoid, talk around, or "pray" about people and situations that should really be dealt with through direct conversation. Ironically, most of us know what the Scriptures say about confrontation and gossip, yet we fail to act upon those biblical directives. Christians are notorious for creating a sliding scale for sin. Gossip and slander are at the bottom of the scale, whereas the "big sins" like fornication, gambling, or drinking are way up there and should be avoided at all costs. We are particularly good at exempting ourselves from what we deem to be smaller sins. It is easy to argue about the infallibility or inerrancy of Scripture—*and hence the need to take Jesus literally*—but we gloss right over Jesus' very clear instructions about how we should deal with confrontation.

Matthew 18, for instance, clearly communicates Jesus' thoughts on interpersonal relationships:

> "If another member of the church sins against you, go and point out the fault when the two of you are alone. If the member listens to you, you have regained that one. But if you are not listened to, take one or two others along with you, so that every word may be confirmed by the evidence of two or three witnesses. If the member refuses to listen to them, tell it to the church; and if the offender refuses to listen even to the church, let such a one be to you as a Gentile and a tax collector."
>
> Matthew 18:15–17

First, Jesus underscores the fact that most of us are *blind* to our own sin. "If another member of the church sins against you," says Jesus. Jesus does not say, "If your brother or sister *intentionally or knowingly* sins against you." Jesus does not say, "When your brother or sister comes to an awareness of their sin against you." The implication of Jesus' statement is that the fellow member is totally unaware that he or she has done anything wrong. Jesus places the responsibility on the individual who is sinned *against*. According to Jesus, the responsibility does not rest upon the one who commits the sin. Like Brian making his sexist remark, the sinner is often blinded and ignorant of his or her offense. The mandate from Jesus is to go privately and point out the fault.

This is one of the reasons why community is so essential. If I commit a sin against someone, there is a good chance that I will be blind to my action. I will need someone to point out my wrong ways. I will need someone to help me see that I have gone astray. If, as Paul claims, the wages of sin is death, then I need someone to pull me off the path to death and get me back on track. This happens best in some kind of community among people who are committed to one another and are willing to take the uncomfortable step of confrontation.

A good friend used to attend a popular megachurch—one that had four services every Sunday. Someone in the church had hurt her deeply by gossiping confidential information about her. Rather than confronting the individual directly, my friend decided to attend the 11:00 A.M. service—the service that the offender did *not* attend. She could avoid the individual who had wronged her.

The sad part of this story is that the woman who committed the offense was oblivious to her sin of gossip. Without someone confronting her directly, she will continue in her blindness to commit the same sin. My friend, on the other hand, will never develop the skill of confrontation—a skill that is difficult for many of us. In a true community the woman could never get away with this action. She would have to confront her friend. She would need to gather up her courage to pull the person aside and lovingly tell her of the wrong. Both people would grow through the experience of confrontation.

We cannot grow as God's children without the truth from others. We cannot develop an awareness of our shortcomings, our sins, or our ignorance without the presence of those who care enough to confront us with love and truth. Friends can be like mirrors reflecting back what we need to see. As the writer of Proverbs 27:17 so vividly states, "As iron sharpens iron, a friend sharpens a friend" (NLT). We need community so others can sharpen us.

But do not think this is an easy process. Healthy, restorative confrontation takes skill and sensitivity. It is not something we learn overnight but a craft that takes practice and fortitude, repetition and courage. But most of us avoid this exercise (I call it *a spiritual exercise* because it is so important for the health of God's work in the world). Without the accountability and commitment of community, we typically run from uncomfortable situations, yet the skill of truthful and loving confrontation is a vital gift to those who truly want to grow in their faith and mature as disciples of Jesus. If we truly commit to a community, we will become leaders who both develop the skill of confrontation and become more aware of our own shortcomings.

Those who grow most in their faith and become successful at developing other people are usually those who exercise the commands of Matthew 18 in their vocational lives. Intellect, personality, GPA, and the school from which they graduate will ultimately have little bearing on their effectiveness as authentic Christian leaders, managers, supervisors, entrepreneurs, and role models. The ability to confront in love and to learn from the confrontation of others—two skills that are learned in community—will determine their effectiveness in these roles.

Community and Calling: One More Time

One reason I encourage students to join a ministry for a year after they graduate from college or university is so they can discover their calling. After spending a year in a ministry community, students usually have a deeper sense of who they are as disciples and a clearer sense of their calling. By living and working together in caring relationship with other people, these students receive valuable insight regarding their gifts and talents.

Unfortunately our modern educational system does not always help students in this area. Students can lock themselves away on campus for four years, read countless books, write too many papers, and take too many exams. They are assessed on the basis of how they retain and absorb data. Seldom are links created between learning and discovering one's calling. Few students get to know each other, really seeing themselves in action—working, relating, and serving. Few people take the time to help students discern their gifts. Yes, partway through our college experience, we dutifully select a major, which is supposed to provide our life direction, yet too many persons end up in jobs that have no relationship to the majors chosen. Something is wrong with the system.

By becoming a part of a community where people watch out for us, mentor us, pray with us, and try to help us discern our calling, we are more apt to start down a positive path that is consistent with our gifts and talents, our true selves, our passions, and our interests.

"But I Don't Like Kids!"

One summer a young man joined our mission to help with our children's programs. He taught art and photography to teenagers. Nick was extremely talented and gifted. By the end of the summer Nick wanted to join our teaching staff. The new school year started with excitement and record numbers of children in our programs.

Two days after the fall programs began, Nick came to my office.

"I don't know quite how to say this," Nick began, "but I've discovered I don't really like kids, and I'm not good at working with them."

"Well now, that *is* a bit of a problem," I said with a trace of impatience, "especially since we *are* a children's ministry."

"I know," replied Nick. "But, I think I *have to* leave."

"What's your plan? What will you do?"

For the next twenty minutes Nick shared how he liked graphic design and production. He also shared how he had experience in silk-screen design. Soon we were discussing the possibility of starting a small screen-printing business, a place where teens learned a trade and gained some work experience. I sensed an excitement beginning to develop in Nick.

When this new possibility for Nick was brought up at our next staff meeting, the others on our team unanimously affirmed it. Everybody wanted Nick to remain within the community. Everybody sensed that this would be a good use of Nick's gifts and talents. With the affirmation of the community, Nick was off and running. Within the next few weeks, Nick built a $40 printing press out of some two-by-fours and an old kitchen counter top, recruited some local teenagers, claimed an abandoned storefront building on Westfield Ave., and launched into his first commercial printing endeavors. His team—a fourteen-year-old nicknamed Apple and a sixteen-year-old named Jamil—produced 10,000 full-color, creative Christmas cards.

In the months leading up to Christmas, our ministry sold those cards for a dollar each. We made $9,000! The money was reinvested and we were off and running. Hallmark cards, watch out!

For the next nine years, Nick built the business into a thriving enterprise. Now Camden Printworks averages $500,000 each year in sales, employs many community adults and teens, and does work for organizations such as Campbell's Soup, Habitat for Humanity, and the House of Blues.

This expression of God's work in the world exists today because a brother was able to find his calling and exercise his gifts. Within the community Nick's gifts were discovered, affirmed, and supported.

The New Testament tells about people finding their sense of calling within community. For example, in the book of Acts one learns of the growth and struggles of the early church. Their initial fellowship of believers grew at such a rapid rate that the apostles could not continue to preach the good news and take care of the needs of the people. As often is the case, *need necessitated change.* Luke records that the Hellenists of the early church began complaining because their widows were being overlooked during food distribution. It probably was not an intentional act of neglect—the apostles were just too busy. When the apostles heard the grumbling of the people, they called a community meeting. "We apostles should spend our time preaching and teaching the word of God, not administering a food program," they said. "Now look around among yourselves, friends, and select seven men who are well respected and are full of the Holy Spirit and wisdom. We will put them in charge of this business. Then we can spend our time in prayer and preaching and teaching the word" (6:2b–4 NLT).

The responsibility was given to the community to find seven people who would be good at responding to widows and the needy in the community. The community was given the charge to make the selection. The community had to discern the gifts of those who could help in the ongoing mission of the church. Not only would a good selection of seven people ensure that no one would go hungry, it would also allow the apostles to continue exercising *their* gifts as preachers and evangelists. From the beginning of the early church, people found their callings in the context of a community.

Luke communicates this idea again in Acts 13. Barnabas and Saul had just returned from their mission in Jerusalem. In the faith community at Anitoch, Barnabas and Saul found fellowship and an opportunity to worship. It is a wonderful image. I can just imagine Saul and Barnabas needing to find a *home* with a community of believers after an exhausting missionary endeavor. How wonderful it must have been to drop into Antioch and find a vibrant and supportive fellowship! And during that visit God spoke through that community of people. Through that community these two men found new direction for the exercising of their calling. "While they were worshiping the Lord and fasting, the Holy Spirit said, 'Set apart for me Barnabas and Saul for the work to which I have called them.' Then after fasting and praying they laid their hands on them and sent them off" (Acts 13:2–5).

Again, the community played a vital part in helping Barnabas and Saul discern their calling and their new mission. God spoke through the community of people. God used the affirmation and spiritual discernment of a group of people to redirect the gifts and talents of Saul and Barnabas.

It would be wrong to say that Christians can find their calling and life direction only within the context of a faith community. Some people discover their passions and the place God wants them to serve without receiving guidance of a caring Christian community. But God does offer this unique and special gift to those who choose to make the commitment of connecting with a community that is interested and concerned about personal decisions. That support can be a tremendous help as one seeks to be faithful to God's calling.

Encouragement for the Long Haul

It was one of those moments I will never forget, the kind of moment one dreams about for years—one of those dreams you are glad to wake from and thank God that it is not real.

It happened during the second semester of my junior year. I had signed up to take a very difficult theology class with the toughest professor on campus. Everybody warned me not to take the class, but I did not heed their advice. Dr. Johnson was notorious for severely critiquing papers and giving difficult lectures. His classes were usually small because most students didn't want to risk their GPAs. Those of us who did take the class quickly bonded. We realized that we were dependent on one another for our survival.

The day came for me to give my oral presentation. I had worked feverishly for a week, trying to prepare a tight presentation, a presentation that would reflect my mastery of my subject: How Surrounding Cultures Influenced the Development of Religious Thought in Israel. I was hyped. I was ready.

Partway through the presentation, Dr. Johnson put up his hand. I froze. Everything had been going well. Students had been listening. Although very nervous, I had been communicating the information clearly. Why was he going to ask a question right in the middle of my presentation?

"Mr. Main," Dr. Johnson cleared his throat, "you have not alluded to the influence of the Babylonian sun god in the poetry of the Psalms. Are you planning to address that issue?"

Babylonian sun god? What Babylonian sun god? If there were a sun god, I had no more idea of a Babylonian sun god than I did of the Japanese language, and certainly not how it influenced the writing of the Psalms! I was speechless. My brain went dead. I was sweating.

"Mr. Main, don't you realize that this is a significant theme? Tell us what you think of the topic," continued the aged professor.

By this time all of my friends had their heads bowed. I was not sure if they were praying for me or if they just could not bear to look at me during this public flogging. I stood there for an eternity. I could say nothing. Fortunately, the buzzer for the end of class sounded. I fled through the door.

I found a bench outside the library and slumped down. I was devastated, humiliated—still shaking. I'm quitting. I'm dropping that class. That wasn't fair. I'll declare a new major. That'll show 'em. I thought every negative thought possible.

"You mind if I join you?" There stood Michael Lumus, a brilliant, confident theology major in his senior year. "Old Johnson just sort of had you for lunch, didn't he?" he began. I nodded sheepishly. "Don't let him get you down," continued Lumus. "That happened to me once. He comes across a little rough, but he does that to people he likes. You'll see."

"Thanks a lot," I responded sarcastically. I was not ready to believe that Dr. Johnson liked me.

"Hey, if you ever need help, just give me a call. Whatever I can do!" concluded my encouraging friend.

At that moment I needed to hear those words—especially from an older brother in the faith whom I respected and admired. Because of Michael I did not drop the class. To my surprise I actually ended up getting a B and took another two classes from old Dr. Johnson. And guess what? When I look back on my college experience, I realize that he was one of the professors from whom I learned the most!

The right words, from the right person, at the right time can make a difference in our lives. A word of encouragement can be just enough to keep a person hopeful during a very difficult time. Furthermore, a word of encouragement can make the difference between quitting and continuing. Peter Gomes, the chaplain at Harvard, articulates this idea wonderfully when he claims, "To live for reward is always to live for success, and when success eludes us, as it often does, so too does reward. We may live 'for' reward, but we live 'by' encouragement, which is what we need when things don't go well. The trick is that we cannot encourage ourselves: even in this self-help culture of ours, we cannot yet do that. We must be encouraged by someone else and it is our spiritual obligation to encourage one another."[49]

Community can create a place where we can find encouragement and where we can encourage others. No one is exempt from the need for encouragement. Where will we find this much-needed support and strength throughout life?

The writer of the book of Hebrews believed that discouraged people could find encouragement within the community of Christian faith. One senses from the early chapters in Hebrews that this community was tired and discouraged. People had fallen away from the faith and endured hardship. To this the writer responded, "And let us consider how to provoke one another to love and good deeds, not neglecting to meet together, as is the habit of some, but encouraging one another, and all the more as you see the Day approaching" (10:24–25). The writer appealed to this group of people to keep gathering together on a regular basis. Keep the community meeting! Regularly! For the way to fight discouragement and hardship is to encourage and stimulate one another.

If Jesus Were a Senior

For many college and university graduates, the difficulty of postcollege life is the loss of wonderful friendships and a sense of community, fellowship clubs, Bible studies, and communal living. Those opportunities provide a wonderful sense of support, but sometimes this disappears at graduation. As the last diploma is passed out and the last trunk packed on move-out day, so also goes the availability of community. Because this absence of fellowship can create a tremendous hole in a person's life, it is important to be thinking about this issue prior to graduation.

A few years ago a group of students from Eastern College had gotten involved with issues of homelessness and poverty during their college years. They went to rallies together to fight for the rights of those without housing, they went into the city on Friday nights to feed people who were hungry, and they mobilized other students on campus to become aware of issues surrounding poverty. Throughout their college years, these students built strong relationships with one another. As graduation approached, they made a commitment to one another: they would move into a very poor section of North Philadelphia and live as a community. They did not want their unique friendships, or their commitment to poor people, to diminish after graduation. They called this community the Simple Way. Those former students lived frugally in a community to demonstrate God's love to their neighbors in North Philadelphia. Their community continues to provide accountability, intimacy, and a place to grow in their faith.

Their motivation was that Jesus believed in community. For three years he surrounded himself with a community of twelve men who traveled together, ate together, prayed together, learned together, and grew in faith together. By building a community around himself, Jesus modeled that the very nature of God's work is communal. Jesus could have worked alone, even lived in a cave by himself. But Jesus intentionally chose to live in partnership with and commitment to other people. That is an important reality as you think about *your* faith—especially after college.

Unfortunately, too many people *discard* their faith after college. They lose their idealism and dreams. One of the reasons this happens is because people never find a community that affirms their values and dreams, nor do they find a group of people with whom they can be vulnerable and with whom they can find accountability. Finding or forming a good community will be one of the most important acts of your life.

A Conversation with Jesus

The dormitory was eerily quiet. Just the day before there had been a buzz of excitement—students packing their clothes, doing their last batch of laundry, and tearing down illegally placed posters from dorm room walls, parents pulling up in front of the dorms in pickup trucks and SUVs. But that had been the day before.

This April was different from the past four years. I would not be coming back. Part of me was ready to move on; another part was saddened by the prospect of not seeing some of my friends again. Sure we would have e-mail. But it would just not be the same. Jim was off to Colorado to work at a youth ranch. Steve was heading oversees with a marketing firm. Linda was off to graduate school in Cambridge.

As I placed the last of my books in a brown corrugated box, I heard the Voice over my shoulder. I continued my work without turning around. "You need some help?"

"Thanks. But I'll be okay. Where were you an hour ago when there was still lots of work to be done," I asked in jest.

"Well, I'm really sorry," replied my Friend, mockingly. *"But someone in the chapel was calling."*

"I understand," I said, trying to recover. *"I'm sure you've been dealing with all kinds of crises and separation anxiety this week."*

I heard the grunt of agreement from behind me. Then he said, *"What are you going to be doing about friendships? Your friends are heading off in all directions this week, and they've been your support for the past few years."*

"I know. I haven't quite figured that one out yet. I was thinking of just walking alone for awhile." There was a pause.

"You may want to rethink that one," continued my Friend. *"When I was walking around down here, I surrounded myself with people who wanted to grow and learn together. Sure, they got on my nerves a bit, and they let me down on occasion, but I chose the companionship. It made a difference for me."*

"Why did you bother with those knuckleheads? It would have been easier to keep your distance from people—you know, keep that celebrity distance?"

"But you're missing the point of how God chooses to work in the world and in people. A Christian doesn't live or thrive in isolation. Imperfect Christians need to be in relationship with other imperfect Christians if they are to move toward becoming the people God wants them to be. Furthermore, God works best through groups of people."

"Oh. I guess most of my lessons and important moments of growth came through relationships. In prayer groups I really learned to pray. Then on mission trips I really learned about community, self-sacrifice, and confrontation. It was in Bible studies that the Scriptures spoke most powerfully to me. Yeah. Communities of people really have made a difference in my life."

But by that time my Friend had gone.

Remember:

The religious community does not fulfill its role in the formation of young adult faith unless it can recognize the gifts of young adults, welcome their emerging competence, and give them power. This, again, is done in part through the power of recognition.
—Sharon Daloz Parks, *Big Questions: Worthy Dreams*

Reflection for Students

1. Do you presently have a community from which you draw support and accountability? Is this important to you? Why is it important to you?

2. What does true community look like? Give an analogy or a metaphor.

3. Do you have any postgraduate plans for community? If so, what are they? If not, why don't you?

4. Do you like church? If so, what in the church's life causes you to like church? If not, what do you not like about church?

5. Where do you think you can find some kind of community after graduation?

For the Leader

1. Ask each of the students to share a situation or story where community has helped encourage them, clarify their callings, or hold them accountable.

2. Ask your students what you can be doing to help them prepare to find community after college.

Meditation

Lord,

Community sometimes frightens me.
It means being real,
    being vulnerable,
    being held accountable and holding others accountable.
It means being confronted and confronting others.
Yet I know I need these things in my life.

Help me to find a place where I can be known;
    a place where my gifts can be used and my talents
    discovered.
Help me to find a place where I can grow,
    where I can keep my vision alive,
    where I can truly be released to do your work in the world.

Protect me from the rugged individualism of this culture,
    from the self-centeredness and isolation that our culture
    breeds.
I don't want to simply be an island.
I want to enjoy and experience the fullness of your community.

Amen

Chapter 9

Portfolio Preparations: Other World Investing

As we begin to understand the true nature of God's reign,
we realize that all our resources belong to that reign.
We realize that giving everything over to God is not a
demand.
Instead, it's an invitation to live in relationship with the
ultimate nature of the universe,
a universe grounded in love.

David Hilfiker

For where your treasure is, there your heart will be also.

Matthew 6:21

No Trumpets

As I was washing the dishes one Sunday afternoon, the TV was on and I caught the tail end of a PBS documentary honoring the recipients of the Jefferson Awards—awards given to ordinary citizens who do extraordinary things. One of the recipients, Art Dawson, really caught my attention.

The announcer reported that for the past forty years Art Dawson had worked for the Ford Motor Company as a forklift operator—working six, sometimes seven, days a week and usually putting in twelve-hour shifts. He had a one-bedroom apartment and a very simple lifestyle. He appeared to be a humble, hardworking, blue-collar kind of guy. Surprisingly, Dawson was being honored as a philanthropist!

Philanthropist? Philanthropists are supposed to be venture capitalist types, men or women who start high-tech businesses and sell them for gazillions of dollars and have stock portfolios as thick as telephone books. Or maybe a highly paid athlete or actor, *lending* their name to a great charity as they make their highly publicized gift.

But not forklift operators with seventh-grade educations, raised in poverty in the backwoods of Louisiana. Certainly *not* the Art Dawsons of the world.

The announcer went on to say, with appropriate excitement in his voice, that over the past ten years Art Dawson had given $1,500,000 in scholarship money to young university students who came from impoverished backgrounds. Every extra dollar Dawson had earned had been saved in an effort to give to others. His choice to live simply, to invest his money in blue-chip stocks, combined with his fierce determination to help others, had made him a significant philanthropist. He had helped hundreds of students—those who never thought they had a dream of going to college—get the kind of education he never had. When asked what had motivated his generosity, he simply said that he wanted to see young people get what he never had—a university degree.

The highlight of the program was listening to the students who had benefited from Art's incredible generosity. Student after student shared how the money for books or tuition made the difference. And they were awed by the source of their scholarships, amazed to discover whom their unusual benefactor was. It gave them increased inspiration and a dedication to study.

After watching that moving segment about Art Dawson, I reflected on what God does through those who love to give—not based on what is *left over* when all our spending is done. Art lived life in reverse; rather than working to get, he worked so he could give.

As the director of an organization that exists because of the benevolence of generous people, I have learned something about people who give. Giving has nothing to do with how much a person possesses or earns. People who give do so regardless of how much they own, how much they make, or how secure their financial situations might be. Giving is an attitude. It is a lifestyle. Giving is a matter of the heart. Giving is a discipline.

Over the years I have met multimillionaires who struggle to part with one dime. But I also have met welfare moms who turn their heat to fifty degrees during the winter and forgo steak for macaroni and cheese, just so they joyously can make an offering to God's work each week. Often notes from my donors are attached to the gifts sent to our mission organization. These remarkable notes tell of heroic generosity. "My husband was just laid off from his job, but we want you to have this little bit of money for the children. I know it is not much, but I hope it helps." Or from the widow on a fixed income, "My heating oil was cheaper this winter; here is what I was able to save." These short notes are incredibly humbling and remind me that there are people who give faithfully and sacrificially and are never noticed.

I am glad that there are also wealthy people who give anonymously and humbly and generously as they choose to live out their faith with little fanfare. They desire no building to be built in their honor, no press release to be sent to the local newspapers, no VIP treatment when visiting the programs they support. The amounts of their dollars are significant, yet no one ever knows of their gifts. They walk away from the seductive temptations of a heightened sense of importance and self-worth. In so doing, they have internalized the words of Jesus, "Whenever you give alms, do not sound a trumpet before you" (Matt. 6:2).

Jesus and Investing

I do not know if Art Dawson's motivation for giving was rooted in a Christian faith conviction. But I do know that Art's attitude toward giving reflects the investment strategy of Jesus, who provides profound advice about how we should handle our money and resources.

Jesus claims: "Do not store up for yourselves treasures on earth, where moth and rust consume and where thieves break in and steal; but store up for yourselves treasures in heaven, where neither moth nor rust consumes and where thieves do not break in and steal. For where your treasure is, there your heart will be also" (Matt. 6:19–21).

Jesus said what so many of us know to be true yet find so difficult to embrace. Storing up things and treasures and impressive portfolios in this life is often a waste of the *precious* and *significant*, for today's top-of-the-line fashions will be sold in thrift stores tomorrow, and the fastest and sleekest cars will be scrap metal in a few years. Nothing on this earth is secure—everything eventually rots or rusts or is left behind. So the challenge Jesus posed was this: invest in things that have value in *heaven!*

What's interesting about Jesus' words is that a few sentences later (6:24) he makes another radical claim, "No one can serve two masters; for a slave will either hate the one and love the other, or be devoted to the one and despise the other. You cannot serve both God and wealth." Basically, Jesus was saying that if your consuming passion is to store up treasures on earth, you couldn't really say you are serving God. For most of us, this idea flies in the face of our culture's dominant, materialistic values.

The Power of Mammon

The late French theologian and social philosopher Jacques Ellul wrote a powerful little book called *Money and Power*. Ellul, usually known for his prophetic insights on technology and the dangers of modern culture, instructs his readers on what the Bible has to say about money and the proper relationship disciples of Jesus should have with this necessity.

One of the central ideas Ellul raises revolves around the question of why Jesus called money *mammon* in both Matthew 6:24 and Luke 16:13. Ellul points out that Jesus did not use a term for money that was popular among his contemporary listeners. Instead, Jesus used a term that *personifies* money, and he considered it a significant god. Ellul states, "This personification of money, this affirmation that we are talking about something that claims divinity . . . reveals something exceptional about money."[50] He argues that money is not a neutral object. Money is not something that just lies dormant in our pockets or purses. Rather, Ellul's argument contends that Jesus used the word *mammon* because he likened money to a *power* or a *force*. Jesus was saying that *mammon* can be a personal master.

At this point one might argue that Ellul is overstating his case and that mammon is an object that has power only over those who make money *a priority* in their lives. But Ellul counters that thinking by claiming, "Jesus is not describing the particular situation of the miser, whose master is money because his soul is perverted. Jesus is not describing a relationship between an object and us, but between an active agent and us. He is not suggesting that we not use money wisely or earn it honestly. He is speaking of a power, which tries to be like God, which makes itself our master and which has specific goals."[51]

Many of us would probably agree that money can be a dangerous and destructive force in people's lives. We have all seen families who have wealth but are dysfunctional and unhappy. But most of us would struggle with the idea that money has "specific goals" and is an "active agent."

If Ellul is correct in his interpretation of Jesus' position on money, how then can the Christian be released from the power of money? One must strip money of its seductiveness and its strength, profane its sacred character. But how? Ellul writes, "There is one act par excellence which profanes money by going directly against the law of money, an act for which money is not made. This act is giving."[52] Just think: in the act of *giving* money loses its control over our lives. Money *loses its power* when we *voluntarily* surrender it to God.

That's probably why Jesus watched how people going in and out of the temple courts gave money. Jesus "watched the crowd putting money into the treasury. Many rich people put in large sums. A poor widow came and dropped in two small copper coins, which are worth a penny" (Mark 12:41). According to Ellul, Jesus was intentional about observing how people dealt with their resources. He watched closely *how* they gave, not the *amount* they gave. He was interested in the way they gave. Jesus applauded the woman who gave "out of her poverty," for she *gave everything she had!* (v. 44) Mammon did not control that woman. She did not serve two masters.

What Is Tithing?

Our postmodern generation often applauds itself on *moving beyond* rigid commitments and stifling rituals, yet the concept of regular giving as *a first priority* is the biblical model. It seems apparent from both the Old and New Testaments that God wants us to develop hearts and minds that think of giving *first*.

The concept of giving a portion—often called a tithe—of what we earn to God as an act of worship is rooted in the Old Testament. For example, in the book of Deuteronomy we read, "Be sure to set aside a tenth of all that your fields produce each year" (14:22 NIV). The writer goes on to record, "Eat the tithe of your grain, new wine and oil, and the firstborn of your herds and flocks in the presence of the LORD your God" (14:33 NIV). We learn that part of the religious life in ancient Israel involved taking a portion of person's earnings (produce and livestock in an agrarian society) and setting them aside for an event that involved the recognition of the Giver of life—God. Over the centuries this idea of setting aside 10 percent for the things of God has become a sort of benchmark for Christian giving. When pastors use the word *tithe*, many associate the word with giving 10 percent of one's income to the church. I imagine that most contemporary Christians think tithing is the weekly practice of putting a few dollars in the offering plates on a Sunday morning.

In Deuteronomy the concept of tithing had nothing to do with giving for the purpose of meeting the general operating expenses of the temple budget or for a new church Sunday school building campaign. This concept of tithe was associated with a *sacred dinner feast*—a party that celebrated the goodness of God and the wonder of God's provision. Tithing was not about dourly and mechanically writing a check at the end of the month to your church—after the bills had been paid. It had nothing to do with trying to appease feelings of guilt through making contributions in the name of God. Tithing in the Old Testament was about a community of people celebrating the miracle of God's involvement in their daily lives.

Later in this passage the concept of the tithe was broadened and took on another dimension. Beyond a meal to celebrate God's goodness, tithing became a communal event to provide for those in need. "At the end of every three years, bring all the tithes of that year's produce and store it in your towns so that . . . the aliens, the fatherless and the widows who live in your towns may come and eat and be satisfied, and so that the LORD your God may bless you in all the work of your hands" (14:28–29 NIV). The collective tithe of the community became a kind of social safety net for the less fortunate in the community and for those who helped with the priestly functions. Deuteronomy reminds us that being one of God's people means sharing in the responsibility of looking after people who have suffered hardship and are struggling to make ends meet. Tithing moves us beyond simply celebrating God's goodness and calls us to share our wealth so that all members of the community can experience provision.

In conclusion, tithing has a dual purpose. First, regular celebrations remind us of God's provision and strip us of our tendency to become self-absorbed and self-reliant. We remember that despite our best efforts and hard work we are simply stewards of God's gifts. Second, tithing is an outward-looking act for the benefit of those who need help.

How should these ancient ideas influence my giving today? Or, more specifically, how much do I need to give? Some Christian leaders claim that we need to give a certain percentage of our income to the work of God. I resist this legalism because it does not capture the essence of discipleship. God never seems to hold people to percentages. *Giving is about the heart.* The theologian and philosopher Austin Farrer once wrote that when it came to the question of giving, we should give until it hurts—until we feel it! He said that when we place our tithe in the offering plate, or give a portion of our resources, we should feel a twinge of pain in our heart. The reason: if our treasure is where our heart is, as Jesus claims, then if it hurts to give, we are reminded that our heart is too attached to our money. Farrer has a point.

I think the apostle Paul's words to the church of Corinth establish a wonderful giving principle. Paul challenges the early disciples of Jesus to move beyond the safety of rules and percentages. Paul presents a much more dynamic and exciting principle when it comes to giving: "The point is this: the one who sows sparingly will also reap sparingly, and the one who sows bountifully will also reap bountifully. Each of you must each give as you have made up your own mind, not reluctantly or under compulsion, for God loves a cheerful giver" (2 Cor. 9:6–7).

Something wonderful happens when we sow generously. In the act of giving beyond what is practical and prudent, our hearts are enlarged, our priorities are altered. We learn to loosen our grip on the enticing, ephemeral things of this world and instead embrace the generous, sacrificial things that are eternal—opening our lives to the potential of reaping generously.

One of the most rewarding aspects of directing a nonprofit ministry is watching people *receive* blessings because of their generous giving. Once a year our ministry sponsors a big fundraising dinner. Our youth gospel choir sings, graduates of the program share their testimonies, and our supporters get to interact with children and teens who participate in our program. People who have faithfully given to our work for years are able to come and meet young people whose lives have been transformed. Our donors always leave the event feeling uplifted and deeply moved. These friends of the ministry see the fruit of the seeds they have planted and receive abundant blessings, blessings that are more valuable than anything they could ever buy with their money.

Nothing encourages me more than getting a phone call from a person who loves to give and wants to use his or her resources to sow generously. One man calls me every few months and asks, "Bruce, are you sleeping at night? I don't want you worrying about finances. What can I do to help?" Phone calls like this keep me going. When the financial needs seem insurmountable, it is reassuring to know that you have generous givers in your corner. Those people rekindle my vision and provide encouragement. They remind me that God does not abandon those who are called to God's work in the world.

Certainly the world needs more people who live to give. Organizations, ministries, and missionaries need people who want to sow generously with their resources. Nonprofit organizations—such as World Vision, Compassion, Youth for Christ, Amnesty International, even UrbanPromise—need faithful people who give a portion of what they earn each month. Organizations like these make a difference in our world. They deal with starvation, third-world development, civil rights, evangelism, and a host of other issues. Most religious organizations do not receive government funding because in so doing they jeopardize their special calling, which may compromise their mission's integrity. But these good works need to grow and prosper. Consequently, we need an up-and-coming generation who will take less for themselves and give more to others.

A Model of Tithing

When I was in college, I worked for a mission organization called Youth for Christ. I had to raise my own support each month to pay my bills and cover program expenses. That was missionary work. I did not get paid unless people sent to the organization money designated for me. No designated money, no food. Waiting for my monthly paycheck was always a nail-biting experience. Would it be $25 or $250? Would I be able to buy vegetables or would it be a month of oodles of noodles? It was a humbling and faith-stretching experience.

One year an international student named Moon found out about my situation and came to me. He was holding out four crisp twenty-dollar bills. "This is for you!" he said.

"Oh, I can't take that. You work too hard, you need it," I responded.

"You must take it! It's my tithe." I was dumbfounded. Moon had very little money. He worked two jobs just to eat and pay his school bills. But, for some reason, he believed in what I was doing with local high school students. Every month I would receive an envelope with four crisp twenty-dollar bills. It was an amazing experience for me. Moon taught me tremendous lessons about giving. For him, giving was linked to his relationship with God and how he was supposed to live out his faith. His giving was sacrificial, but it gave him great joy.

Joyous giving is an essential part of being a Christian. It is an act of worship different from any other. Giving enriches the development of our heart. And without ongoing giving it is easy for the power of money to harden our heart.

How Will You Invest?

The Christian community often provides role models who are "spiritual superstars." Mother Teresa of Calcutta is uplifted as a role model of sacrificial service. Billy Graham is a role model of a person who wins people to Jesus. A talented pastor such as Bill Hybels at Willow Creek Community Church in Illinois is celebrated as a pioneer in church growth. These are wonderful and important people within the Christian community. But these people can be detached from the day-to-day world of many Christians, Christians who wake up every morning and try to live out their faith in the workplace. These day-to-day workers must deal with the realities of earning a living, meeting the bottom line, managing stock portfolios, and negotiating business transactions. Can a Christian be successful in this world, where money is such a dominant theme, and not be seduced by the power of *mammon*? Can a person spend most of his or her life energies in the public sphere and still do things of eternal significance?

Few people have ever heard of the Tappan brothers. They were born in the late 1780s into a large family in Northampton, Massachusetts. Lewis and Arthur became very rich, very influential, and very prominent businessmen in New York City. Arthur made his money in the silk industry and developed one of the largest companies in the country. His success was built upon absolute honesty and a new system of what was called "fixed prices." Lewis set up the Mercantile Agency, which provided credit ratings for businesses across the country. Many feel that his company was instrumental in providing stability for the American economy during the country's critical stage of development. The brothers were known for their honesty and moral character.

But Lewis and Arthur were more than Christian businessmen who embraced moral and ethical business practices—for people could have those values without being Christian. Their faith ran deeper than simple piety and belief in a doctrine that assured them a place in the next life. The Tappan brothers believed that their faith called them to use their resources and status to change society and make it more just for all people. Christian faith, for the Tappan brothers, called them to be social reformers.

Their wealth and lifestyle did not distract them from their mission in life. They did not live extravagantly. In fact they believed that they were *stewards* of God's money. Because of their beliefs they threw themselves and their finances into causes that helped bring about the presence of God's reign in the world. They were major supporters of their contemporary, the well-known evangelist and writer Charles G. Finney. They supported the "free church" movement, which was the creation of a number of new churches that did not exclude the poor because they could not pay for pew space. (Paying for a reserved seat was a common practice in many churches in that day.) Moreover, Arthur and Lewis Tappan were outspoken reformers of the slave trade—often at great personal and financial costs to their businesses. They helped form the New York Anti-Slavery Society in 1833, paying for the legal defense of slaves who were captured on the *Amistad*. (If you remember the history of the time—or if you saw the film *Amistad*—you know that the *Amistad* was a boat built for the slave trade. While transporting slaves from Cuba to Granada, the slaves mutinied, killing the captain and imprisoning the Cuban crew. The United States seized the ship near Long Island. It was those mutineers whom the Tappan brothers helped.)

They also were instrumental in the creation of Oberlin College. Oberlin involved itself in the Underground Railroad and initiated trips to the South to free slaves. The Tappan brothers mandated that Oberlin accept whites and blacks on equal merit. This was revolutionary for the day. This was a radical expression of faith, since the majority of American Christians supported the slave trade.

In 1869 Lewis Tappan authored a pamphlet entitled *Is It Right to Be Rich?* in which he questioned the irresponsible accumulation of wealth in the post–Civil War era. Church historian Donald Dayton claims emphatically, "All of their lives the Tappans plowed most of their wealth back into various philanthropies, benevolent societies, and social reform movements."[53] Even when things got extremely difficult—their silk business experienced a devastating fire and went under in the financial collapse of 1837, people threatened their lives because of their counter-cultural positions, and companies boycotted their businesses—their commitment to God's work in the world did not waver and was never put on hold. The investment strategy of the Tappan brothers was not to accumulate things that "will rot and rust." Their investment strategy was built around seeking first the reign of God *in this world.* Their imaginative and creative giving and tireless efforts changed the political and social landscape of their time.

Our country needs young entrepreneurs like the Tappan brothers—business-savvy men and women who view their jobs as a platform for doing eternal things in the world. The body of Christ needs a new generation of social reformers who *live to give.*

Investing in a Promise

A good friend of mine once bought some strange real estate. Everybody thought Hart was crazy. And, from a worldly point of view, Hart was crazy when he bought a drug-saturated brothel in the worst part of East Vancouver, British Columbia, Canada. Vancouver may be known for its scenic mountains and beautiful ocean views, but there are areas of tremendous need—and this definitely was one.

The three-story boarding house was notorious for crime. The previous owner had made thousands of dollars pimping for women and men in the rooms. Teens would go in and out of the complex for drugs—day and night. Some died of overdoses in the rooms that were used for shooting up heroin, and every night police made arrests. The place was beyond dirty, smelled of human feces, and was dangerous. It certainly was not prime real estate. Florida swampland looked better.

But Hart was on a spiritual journey. For years he had successfully worked to accumulate wealth through real estate deals. But after a while he began to explore the deeper dimensions of his faith. He began to see that he could use his real estate expertise to make a difference in the world for God. And God surprisingly led him to the brothel in East Vancouver.

I remember my first visit to the boarding house. Hart had just bought the facility. As we walked through the halls, I could feel the oppressive spirit. Bathrooms without doors were nothing more than a filthy toilet. The lights—when they worked—were dim bulbs on frayed wires. Windows were broken, paint had pealed. The place was a shambles. "Got a little house cleaning to do, don't you think?" said my friend through a smile as he showed me around.

For the rest of the tour he shared the vision God had given him for the broken-down tenement: rooms would be painted, bathrooms replaced with state-of-the-art fixtures and showers, windows added; twenty-four-hour security would be provided.

"My dream is to create good, safe, clean housing for poor men and women," Hart said with tangible excitement. "Downstairs we'll have counseling offices staffed by church volunteers. People will get help for their living problems and their addictions."

A year later the dream was a reality! The boarding house had been transformed into a beautiful, welcoming place for people. Christians staffed it. And the tenants knew that a miracle had taken place. What was even more interesting was that civic leaders stood in awe of what had been accomplished by *one man with a vision*. The police and politicians were thrilled. Now, other entrepreneurs were waking up to the reality that they could make a difference in their community when they chose to invest in something of significance—something that helps others.

Sure, Hart could have invested in Palm Springs, could have continued to amass a fortune and buy things that he didn't need. But he chose to make another kind of investment. Hart chose to *diversify* his portfolio with investments that reflect the nature of God and the nature of God's vision for a better world. Hart's investments became eternal investments—investments that made a difference in people's lives.

Investing with a Conscience

There is another piece to this investment equation that young Christians should ponder as they begin to think about what they will do if they have any excess money. (It may be a stretch to even imagine such a thing at this point in your life.) But in his book *Corporate Irresponsibility: America's Newest Export*, Lawrence E. Mitchell makes an important observation about American investing practices. Mitchell argues persuasively that American investors seem to feel no moral responsibility for the stock investments they hold. He points out two main reasons for this occurrence.

First, most American investors are committed to short-term gratification when it comes to investing. Because most investors own small amounts of stock, they have limited liability when it comes to the companies in which they own stock. Because of this limited liability, stockholders are not liable for things companies do. So, if a company pours toxic waste into rivers and lakes, the investors feel no responsibility for these destructive actions. If a stock begins to lose value because of a civil case, the investor simply sells the stock, accepting no responsibility for any amoral or negligent actions by the company managers.

Second, even in the case of mutual funds, where a person spreads investment risk over many companies, Mitchell again points out, the average investor remains ignorant and passive about what is taking place in those companies; even retirement pension funds are concerned about only short-term gains, not long-term investments that will benefit our society. To Mitchell, we need investors who will tolerate and encourage the pursuit of long-term strategies and have no real interest in short-term payoff. This would free corporate managers to do the right thing, as opposed to being slaves to the short-term interests of stockholders.

Usually the heart of the problem is the sin of greed. Greed fuels an insatiable desire to make money, regardless of the cost to society or to the environment. For Christians the problem goes beyond greed; it is linked to the compartmentalization of one's faith. Too often we see no connection between our investment strategy and our faith. Too easily Christians buy into a secular/sacred division of life. We have our "spiritual" lives and we have our "real" lives. Consequently, we do not view the companies in which we invest through the lens of a biblical faith; they're not companies that make the world a better place. To divorce faith from investment practices is wrong and unbiblical.

Assuredly, we can invest in companies that promote values consistent with the values of the Christian faith: companies that research and create new technologies and services that make life better for people; companies that are environmentally compliant and work to better our air and water; mutual funds that don't invest in companies that produce tobacco products or use child labor.

Christians are called to be wise and thoughtful investors. Our motives for investing must extend beyond the promise of financial return. We must believe that our investment practices matter and do make a difference in the world.

If Jesus Were a Senior

Even though Americans are living longer—seventy, eighty, ninety years—you probably don't know a lot of one-hundred-year-olds. And you probably don't know what these people think or feel or what their lives were like when they were young. Several years ago there was a survey of that centenarian population, those born at the turn of the century. The group had all outlived their peers and, by their accounts, had been through a unique era—the stock market crash, the Great Depression, and two world wars. They had a first ride in the newly invented automobile, became dependent on electricity, and even had a TV that showed a man taking a step on the moon. They had experienced and benefited from wondrous medical discoveries and advances. They felt they had lived full, wondrous lives. And indeed they had.

After all that, the research team asked the following simple yet profound question: If you could live your life over, what would you do differently? After recording the interviews, the team identified the dominant themes. If given the chance to live their life over again, the individuals said they would risk more, reflect more, and invest in things of eternal significance.

The first response was a surprise. People who had lived a long time wished they had *taken more chances.* They felt they had lived life too cautiously and been governed by fear, rather than living a life of potential and promise. We, like the survey population, can limit our lives to the safe and secure. The centenarians cautioned against that kind of life.

The idea that many of us are far too busy to ever *think about who we are or what we are about* was another profound insight. Where are we going? what are we doing? and what have we done with our lives?—these tend to be threatening questions. Yet the questions and reflections are vital if we want to break out of numbing routines and unhealthy patterns. True reflection causes us to reassess our lives and reevaluate vocation, relationships, and God. The catch is that reflection is difficult and challenging.

Naturally, the third conclusion of the study intrigued me. Some of the people surveyed had acquired tremendous amounts of property or thick and diversified stock portfolios; others had held prestigious positions or enjoyed meaningful careers. Yet many of the centenarians wished they had spent more time *investing in things that would last.* Temporal accomplishments, after a century of living it seems, did not matter much to those people. But why bring up the reflections of the elderly when one is just getting started in life?

It is critical to think about investing at this stage in life because our investments define the kind of life we will live. Jesus was direct in his statements about the priorities we choose for our lives. Jesus wanted his followers to see the absurdity of chasing after material things and focus on investments that would make a difference in the world and lead to a healthier, more vibrant life. Jesus prophetically announced,

Therefore I tell you, do not worry about your life, what you will eat or what you will drink, or about your body, what you will wear. Is not life more than food, and the body more than clothing? Look at the birds of the air; they neither sow nor reap nor gather into barns, and yet your heavenly Father feeds them. Are you not of more value than they? And can any of you by worrying add a single hour to your span of life? And why do you worry about clothing? Consider the lilies of the field, how they grow; they neither toil nor spin, yet I tell you, even Solomon in all his glory was not clothed like one of these. But if God so clothes the grass of field, which is alive today and tomorrow is thrown into the oven, will he not much more clothe you—you of little faith? Therefore do not worry, saying, 'What will we eat?' or 'What will we drink?' or 'What will we wear?' For it is the Gentiles who strive for all these things; and indeed your heavenly Father knows that you need all these things. But strive first for the kingdom of God and his righteousness, and all these things will be given to you as well.

So do not worry about tomorrow, for tomorrow will bring worries of its own. Today's trouble is enough for today.

Matthew 6:25–34

Jesus emphatically and clearly revealed the important things in this life. Jesus helped his disciples to see beyond what the world deems important and laid down a new set of priorities and values. Jesus promised that the anxiety and fear associated with worrying about worldly stuff can be replaced with the confidence of God's provision. And yet there is a command attached to this promise. The command is to *seek first* the witness of God's work and justice in the world. This is the No. 1 investment the disciples of Jesus should make with their lives.

A Conversation with Jesus

I glanced at my watch. With a forty-five-minute break before my next class I decided to take a little detour into the library. Heading directly toward the magazines and periodicals section, I scooped off the rack the latest copies of Fortune, Consumer Reports, *and* Auto Trader *and looked for an empty study booth.*

In a few short weeks I would have my diploma in hand and would be looking for work. I would need a few new "toys" to help my transition into the real world—a new car to get back and forth to the job would be

*great, a cell phone with no roaming charges would be an absolute neces-
sity, and a new laptop computer would allow me to work from home. Oh,
OK, yes, an electronic Palm Pilot would be essential. With good credit
and minimum balances on my credit cards, I knew I would have little
problem securing my desires. My monthly paychecks would at least cover
the minimum credit card payments and car loan. I began to leaf through
the pages and salivate over the glossy pictures of the fastest and finest in
human technology.*

*"What will you get first?" came a Voice from the next study booth. I was
caught off guard. I could not believe that somebody had the audacity to
interrupt my solitude. Then I recognized the Voice.*

*"I'm just doing a little preparation, a little dreaming," came my less-
than-enthusiastic response.*

*"Why get yourself in debt?" asked my Friend. "If you buy all those must-
have fantasies, you'll need to work extra hours just to make payments.
Are you sure this is what you want to do with your time?"*

*I had not really thought about the question. I figured these were neces-
sities. After all, it seemed that everyone else had these things. "But why
can't I enjoy these things?" I asked, with sort of a whine in my voice.*

*"I'm not making a moral judgment about whether you should own a
laptop or a Palm Pilot," came his gentle response. "I just wanted you to
be aware that it's easy to become a slave to credit card companies. Pretty
soon you'll become addicted. Your time will not be your own."*

*By this time I was listening. I had not looked at things from that per-
spective. The Voice continued, "It is a question about investment. Do you
want to spend your best time and your best energy investing in things
that will be cast aside in a few years? Why not invest your time in things
that will last forever? Why not invest in things that will change lives
and change the world?"*

"Forever? What do you mean forever?"

*"Well," he said wistfully, "you've only got so many years to live on this
planet, only so many hours each day. You'll create only so much money
during your lifetime—a lot, or not so much, it doesn't matter. How do
you want to invest those things? If you invest in my work and my purposes, your investment will have an eternal quality. Those kinds of
investments will live even beyond your lifetime."*

*I pondered the statement. After a long pause I closed the magazine and
quietly reflected. My Friend was right. When it was time to leave this*

planet, did I really want a garage full of old computers and outdated junk? Did I really want to spend my life just trying to keep the debt collectors away? I knew people who worked seventy hours a week just so they could keep up with their bills. Sure they had nice cars, big screen TVs, and fancy computers, but they had little time for their families, nor did they have time to volunteer or invest in things that matter to God. That was not what I wanted for my life.

"I need to give that some serious thought," I responded. Silence. I was alone.

Remember:

Americans need rest, and they need to be reminded that they do not cause the grain to grow and that their greatest fulfillment does not come through the acquisition of material things. Moreover, the planet needs a rest from human plucking and burning and buying and selling.

Dorothy Bass, *Practicing Our Faith*

Reflections for Students

1. What is your family's attitude toward money? Do you embrace this attitude? Does this attitude conflict with the biblical attitude toward money?

2. How have you witnessed the destructive force of money in people's lives? How have you witnessed the redemptive force of money in people's lives?

3. What stands in the way of your becoming a person who gives generously? Do you have anxiety or fear about providing for yourself?

4. What kind of giving practices do you exercise right now in your life? Do you think those practices align themselves with what Jesus or Paul suggests when it comes to giving?

5. How will you protect yourself from becoming a person who invests in things that are temporal? What kinds of investments do you hope to make with your life?

For the Leader

1. Ask the students in your group each to share about someone who embodies the spirit of giving generously and joyfully. How do these people give? What do they give to? Ask the students also to share about someone who does not embody the

spirit of generous giving. What restricts these people from giving? How does this inability to give impact their personality?

2. Ask the students to identify different ways they can become generous givers.

Meditation

Lord,

I confess that I hold things too tightly,
    that I give too sparingly,
    that I worry about having enough.
I can be pretty selfish.

Release me from my fears and anxiety about the future.
Replace my fears with the confidence that
    you will provide and meet my needs.
Replace my anxiety with the assurance that
    you take care of your children.

Give me the boldness passionately and generously to invest in
    things that matter to you.
I want to be like the farmer who sows generously and scatters
    the seed far and wide.
May the seed I sow give birth to wonderful expressions of your
    witness in this world.
I pray for a fruitful life—a life that blesses others.
I pray that I may *live to give.*

Amen

Conclusion:
Final Preparations

Difficult and painful as it is,
we must walk on in the days ahead with an audacious faith
in the future.
When our days become dreary with low hovering clouds of
despair,
and when our nights become darker than a thousand
midnights,
let us remember that there is a creative force in this universe,
working to pull down the gigantic mountains of evil;
a power that is able to make a way out of no way
and transform dark yesterdays into bright tomorrows.
Martin Luther King Jr.

Our Lives Matter

Rosa was calling me from an office building in Chicago. She sounded a little lonely and somewhat wistful. "If it weren't for that day outside my school when Judy put a flyer in my hand," she said, "I don't know where I'd be today." She paused for a moment and then said with great feeling, "*I sure wouldn't be here*. I'd never even have heard of Howard University."

I remembered this vivacious young woman as an awkward seventh-grader and later as a teenager who struggled with depression and a fragile sense of self. I remembered that her father had succumbed to drugs, that her mother had lost the struggle to keep the family together, and that her teen sister had again become pregnant.

Given all of her turmoil, it never would have occurred to Rosa that she was smart enough for college. No one in her family had ever finished high school. Why would it be any different for her?

But now—miracle of miracles—Rosa was a college junior and had been selected from an elite group of students to do a summer internship with a large insurance company in the Midwest. "I can't believe it," she continued, reveling in every moment. "They *flew* me out here! I was so excited. And then they picked me up in a stretch limo at O'Hare. And, believe this, now I'm staying in a condo with a Jacuzzi, a huge swimming pool, and maid service! Bruce, it's unreal. They even do my laundry! And I get fresh towels *every day*."

"Hooray for you, Rosa!" I said, remembering that only a few months ago she was discouraged and ready to drop out of college. She could barely even afford to make her tuition payments. This was quite a contrast for a kid from the inner city.

Talking as fast as she could, she effervesced, "You won't believe this, Bruce, but last weekend they took us horseback riding! I've never been on a horse before and, sure, I still ache—but it was *fantastic*."

We talked a while longer, but despite her dramatic new experiences, Rosa, in the midst of all her new world, expressed a deep sadness about her family. "They're laying a guilt trip on me for not being home and helping." She struggled with whether she was doing the right thing. "You know it's tough sometimes," she continued with a catch in her throat. "All the other interns have parents and brothers and sisters who come to visit on weekends. . . . It just gets lonely sometimes, Bruce."

As we hung up, one statement just hung in the air—"If it weren't for Judy's putting a flyer in my hand that afternoon, *I don't know where I'd be today*."

Judy? I tried to remember Judy and put a face to her name, but I couldn't. Judy had been one of the hundreds of college volunteers who helped out our ministry. But despite her anonymity, this forgotten volunteer had significantly altered the course of Rosa's life in that defining moment, placing Rosa on a new path. God used Judy to change Rosa's life.

I often share this story with my staff because it illustrates the importance and significance of our actions—even simple actions that we think are meaningless and incidental. Just think, one afternoon many years ago Judy, instead of taking a nap, or going to the mall, or reading a book, went the extra mile. She stood outside a local elementary school and invited children to join our ministry. Because of Judy's commitment—her selfless initiative—the whole course of Rosa's life had been altered. The flyer that ended up in Rosa's hand turned her in the direction of our ministry. She started coming to our summer camps. When she turned fourteen, she got a job with our employment program and joined a Bible study. At sixteen, we sent her on a college tour. At seventeen, she studied for her SATs with our caring staff. At eighteen, she was introduced to a donor who helped underwrite a portion of her tuition. Many people encouraged and helped Rosa along the way. But it all started with Judy's willingness to pass out flyers to some inner-city children one afternoon.

Do Our Actions Matter?

How much do our actions matter? Did Judy's decision to pass out flyers rather than take a nap really make the difference in lifting Rosa out of a life of struggle and potential underachievement? Would Rosa's life be completely different today if she had not received that little slip of paper?

Sometimes Christians give too much responsibility to God and too little responsibility to themselves. But over the years I have heard volunteers say after a few days of work in the inner city, especially after it's been 100 degrees all week, and always with tears in their eyes, "I think I need to move on—I know that God will take care of these kids." This demonstrates the person's complete lack of understanding of the role of human beings in God's redemptive plan. Those students believe that their commitments, their actions, and their decisions have little impact on what happens in the world. They wrongly believe that "*God* will take care of things."

The reality is that God does *not* take care of those kids whom *we* are called to take care of. Rather, those kids' lives are profoundly impacted by the *absence* of a caring adult. They are not magically mentored; they are not nurtured by some computer they sit in front of between three and six each day. Those kids, whom we think—or hope—God is supposed to take care of, end up getting abused, dropping out of school, selling drugs, or getting pregnant because there was no caring, committed person in their lives. God relies on us to carry out works of grace, love, and justice in the world.

The movie *Schindler's List* is a powerful portrayal of the significance of one human life. Oskar Schindler, because of his creative willingness to risk his own life to save others, managed to save thousands of Jews from extermination in World War II. He did not turn a blind eye to the problems that resulted from a distorted nationalism and racial bigotry. He did not believe that somehow *God* would supernaturally take care of the Jewish people.

At the end of the film there was a stunningly dramatic moment. After the Germans had lost the war, Jews were finally being released from devastatingly evil prison camps. Schindler was there, surrounded by throngs of emaciated, barely surviving shadows of men and women who were thanking him for saving their lives. During that moment, a moment that should have been a celebration, Schindler realized that he could have done more—*he could have saved more lives.* The weight of that responsibility overwhelmed him. He began to sob uncontrollably while slowly slipping off his ring, "If only I had sold it, *if only I had sold it,*" he said with enormous anguish. "I could have saved another ten people." He looked at the material things that he had held on to—his watch, his car, his coat—and realized that that money could have all been used to save other people. The weight of his grief was overwhelming.

How much do *our* actions matter? What is the relationship between God's activity and our commitments and choices? How much do we limit God's actions because of *our* decisions, *our* laziness, *our* selfishness?

Austin Farrer, a British theologian, argued persuasively that God works in the world when the divine intentions are coupled with human intentions. He called it a theology of the *double will.* In effect, when the divine will and the human will combine, God's movement and presence can truly be released to move in the world. His strong point was that *both wills are needed.* When people combine their commitment, their passion, and their creativity with the Spirit and intentions of God, great and wonderful things take place.

Converging Lines of Faithfulness

James Fowler provides an interesting metaphor for understanding how God interfaces with our human decisions. Fowler looked at a historical event like the civil rights movement and saw God in that movement—for it was a movement toward justice and liberation in our country, the process of unmasking an evil system. But God moved through human beings to bring about a massive social change.

Fowler claims that people often identify a leader like Martin Luther King Jr. as the instrument that God used to really expose the evils of racism. Fowler does not negate the importance of a man like King, but he also believes that God's presence in that movement was linked to the faithfulness and courage of thousands of others who lived *before* King. Fowler writes, "We see the persons who stood behind them [King] for generations back. We see the influence of teachers and mentors brought together with them at crucial moments for some element of preparation and development that would be decisive in an as yet unanticipated future."[54]

What Fowler underscores is that King's emergence and success as a dynamic leader was directly linked to the lives of other faithful people—people who mentored King, people who taught King, and people who had been faithfully chipping away at the walls of a racist society for years. According to Fowler, there was a *convergence* of many lives in the life of Dr. King. Fowler writes: "Such factors as these begin to make visible to us how the divine praxis draws together long lines of convergent faithfulness in order to bring about redemptive transformation in the midst of peoples and of history. And they lead us to reflect how faithfulness in our vocations may contribute—far beyond any set of connections we can now see or imagine."[55]

Picture it this way. Think of a roaring river—its energy, force, and awesome ability to change and alter a landscape. Follow that river upstream. Go farther and you will see that the roaring river divides into smaller rivers. As you trace some of the smaller rivers, you will realize that they also divide and become yet smaller. The roaring river is really a collection of smaller streams. The cascading river you first visualized is simply the final expression of hundreds of tributaries that have mounted in force and power.

Fowler encourages Christians to view themselves as these tributaries. As each of us walks in faithfulness, seeking God's witness and justice in the world, our efforts combine with others on the same journey. Our *converging lines of faithfulness*—dynamic expressions of God's presence and movement—become visible in the world, for our lives and actions are connected to bigger movements of God in the world. When *we* fail to walk faithfully, a tributary is blocked and fails to connect with the other tributaries of faithfulness. Who knows how our lack of faithfulness will impact the future movements of God? Who knows how many lives will indirectly, or directly, be impacted because of our selfishness or our disobedience? Fowler's metaphor shows that the way we live our lives matters. Our choices, our actions make a difference to others and God.

It is critically and eternally important for us to make a series of continuous decisions that are informed and guided by God's Spirit.

Hold On to the String

George MacDonald—one of my favorite children's authors—provides another helpful metaphor for those who want to make good decisions. In a wonderful little story called *The Princess and the Goblin*, a young boy named Curdie is given a very special gift. Curdie is a poor miner boy who finds himself with the daunting task of trying to rescue a princess who has been kidnapped by a bunch of goblinlike creatures who live in underground caves—old mining caves. Curdie cannot fulfill this task by himself.

Fortunately Curdie is given a gift from a Christlike figure, a mystical grandmother who spends her days weaving at a magical spinning wheel. The gift? When Curdie puts his thumb and forefinger together he feels a piece of thread. The grandmother tells him that he will find guidance out of difficult circumstances when he puts his thumb and forefinger together and follows this thread. If Curdie trusts the direction in which the thread leads, the grandmother promises deliverance from harm and assures him that he will ultimately be led back to her at the spinning wheel.

Sure enough, Curdie finds himself rescuing the abducted princess and must find their way out of the underground cave system. These caves are dark and confusing, and goblins are chasing him. Curdie becomes afraid but then remembers the grandmother's words. He places his thumb and finger together and feels the piece of thread! He begins to follow the path of the thread as it leads both the princess and him through the caves. But it is not easy for Curdie to follow the string. When it takes him in directions that seem to contradict his logic and common sense, Curdie wants to let go of the string. But he decides to trust. Curdie decides to walk ahead and trust the word of the grandmother at the spinning wheel. Eventually Curdie finds a way out of the cave to safety.

MacDonald's illustration is a powerful reminder for all people who want faithfully to follow God's leading. At times "following the thread" can defy human reason and cut against our common sense. The tunnels may be long and dark, and we may not see any light. We may take an unexpected turn. But we must hang on to "the thread"—the intentions of God for our lives—and believe that by listening and trusting and serving God we will ultimately find wholeness and abundant life.

Final Preparations

Jesus' message and movement have lived on and on over the centuries. The message of Christian faith and the Spirit of God have been carried by men and women who have committed their lives to being disciples of Jesus. These disciples have had different shapes, different personalities, different ethnicities, and different backgrounds. Some have lived short and fruitful lives, while others have been blessed with long lives. Regardless, broken, fallible, human beings have been used to carry out the work of God in the world. Sure, there are moments of miraculous intervention, but the majority of God's work is made manifest through ordinary human beings.

It is the rather ordinary man Abraham and the aging, beyond-childbearing-age Sarah whom God calls to be the father and mother of the people of Israel. It is the excuse-making, speech-impaired, ordinary man Moses whom God uses to deliver Israel from Egyptian captivity. It is the young boy Samuel whom God calls to become a prophet and leader for Israel. It is the orphan Esther who steps out in courage and convinces King Ahasuerus not to kill her people. It is the shepherd from Tekoa, Amos, whom God calls to confront Israel concerning its injustice and improper treatment of the poor. It is the teenage girl Mary whom God uses to birth Jesus. And it is the ragtag group of fishermen whom Jesus calls to be the foundation of his movement. The history of God's moving in the world is full of ordinary, imperfect people responding faithfully to the call of God in their lives.

I believe that in today's generation of young adults there are the new Moseses, Esthers, Amoses, and disciples. God needs leaders. God needs people who will walk with faithfulness. God needs young adults who will begin the process of preparing for the future—putting in place the needed behaviors that will help keep them focused and growing in faith.

Who knows what you will be doing ten years from now? You may become a dynamic teacher who pours his heart into hurting students. You may become a manufacturer who cares first for God's creation and your employees, making the bottom line secondary. You may become a doctor who gives her time and talents to bring health and well-being to the people who cannot otherwise enjoy quality medical services. You may become a venture capitalist who gives generously and pours his money and resources back into God's work in the world. You may become a mother or father of a loving family. Whatever vocation you chose, it is critical that what you do becomes an extension of your faith and discipleship. As faithful followers of Jesus, it is essential that we be clothed in the compassion, justice, and truth of God.

So whether you will graduate from a prestigious university or a less-well-known college, enter the *real world* with your eyes wide open to the realities you will face. Jesus' prayer for his disciples as he was about to leave them is a sobering reminder of what may lie ahead: "I have given them your word, and the world has hated them because they do not belong to the world, just as I do not belong to the world. I am not asking you to take them out of the world, but I ask you to keep them safe from the evil one" (John 17:14–15). So with the reality of evil lurking around the corner and the potential resistance to your good works always near, take comfort that you are sent out into the world with the promise of God's protection, provision, and grace.

Walk faithfully.

May your life bear much fruit.

A Conversation with Jesus

I had dreamed of this day since high school. I could hear my name announced over the public address system. I walked across the stage in front of my fellow students and parents and shook the hand of the president of the college. And now that day had arrived! Yet I just needed to close my eyes for a moment. *As I sat and listened to the commencement speaker drone on, my eyelids began to close. I really wanted to be alert and absorb the details of the day, but the hot sun, the black robe, and a week of finals. . . . I knew I was supposed to listen and be inspired, but . . . I . . . just . . . kept . . . fading . . .*

"Are you prepared?" I was startled. I knew that Voice. It was the Voice that has guided me for the last few years. It was the Voice that has given me comfort and advice (even when I did not ask). It was the Voice that provided direction.

"Prepared . . . prepared . . . for what?" I asked.

"Well, are you prepared for this important next step?" After four years of classes, term papers, and exams, sure, I was ready to put some of my

head knowledge into practice. I was excited about the next steps. I still didn't know exactly what I would be doing next, but I had a growing sense of calling. And I knew there was another dimension to my Friend's question. I waited for more.

"Yes, I think you are prepared." An incredible wave of calmness ran over me. "You have used these years well. You have solidified your values. You have discovered some of your special gifts and passions. You have dared to dream and have put yourself in situations where your faith has been stretched."

"Thanks," I responded, feeling really good. "But where am I going? What's the next step?"

"Don't be so anxious. I'll lead you. It won't always be clear, and the path won't always be straight and easy, but I will lead you! But stay close to me. And remember, your decisions matter. They make a difference!"

I wanted to talk some more. But just then I heard someone say my name. I rubbed my eyes and realized that the time had come. Standing as tall and proud as I could, I walked to the podium.

Remember:

The great spiritual task facing me is to so fully trust that I belong to God that I can be free in the world—free to speak even when my words are not received; free to act even when my actions are criticized, ridiculed, or considered useless; free also to receive love from people and to be grateful for all the signs of God's presence in the world. I am convinced that I will truly be able to love the world when I fully believe that I am loved far beyond its boundaries.

Henri Nouwen, *Beyond the Mirror*

Reflections for Students

1. In what ways have your prepared yourself academically and spiritually for graduation and life after college?

2. What are your greatest fears about life after college?

3. What excites you most about life after college?

4. Do you really believe that your decisions and actions can make a difference in the world? If so, what kind of contribution do you want to make to God's work in the world?

For the Leader

Your students return for a class reunion in ten years. Have them respond to the following questions, asked by an old classmate:

1. How does your faith inform your daily life? How does it impact the way you do your job?
2. What kinds of investments have you made over the past decade? How have these investments helped others? How have they made a difference in the world?
3. If I asked one of your coworkers or employees to describe you—what would you want them to say about you?

Meditation

Lord,

Thank you for these last few years—
  times of learning, times of reflecting, and times of growing.

I confess that I am a little uncertain about this next chapter of life—where I will go, whom I will meet, and what I am to become.

As I take these next steps, I seek guidance, wisdom,
  and the presence of your Spirit in all my decisions.

Help me to never forget that my choices matter,
  that my life is significant and can—in a large or small way—
  make a difference in this world.

Peel away those insecurities, self doubts, and fears that blind me
  from understanding whom I am created to become—
  and help me to celebrate my unique gifts, my one-of-a-kind
  history, and my sometimes quirky personality, knowing your
  Spirit can redeem these pieces of my being for your work in
  the world.

And please, grant me the energy, the courage, the vision, and
      the integrity
  to live as your disciple each day, always taking the way of
      the cross
  and showering those I meet with your love and
      compassion.

Amen.

Take my life, and let it be consecrated, Lord, to thee;
Take my hands, and let them move at the impulse of thy love.
Take my feet, and let them be swift and beautiful for thee;
Take my voice, and let me sing always, only, for my king.
Take my lips, and let them be filled with messages from thee;
Take my silver and my gold; not a mite would I withhold.
Take my love, my God; I pour at thy feet its treasure store;
Take myself, and I will be ever, only, all for thee.

Frances R. Havergal

Notes

1. Annie Dillard, *Teaching a Stone to Talk: Expeditions and Encounters* (New York: Harper & Row, 1982), 24–25.
2. Alexandra Robbins and Abby Wilner, *Quarterlife Crisis: The Unique Challenges of Life in Your Twenties* (New York: Putnam, 2001), 2–3.
3. Robbins and Wilner, 3.
4. Robbins and Wilner, 3.
5. UrbanPromise Ministries seeks to equip inner-city children and teens with the skills necessary for academic achievement, life management, spiritual growth, and Christian leadership. This mission is fulfilled through the creation of neighborhood-based summer camps, teen employment programs, alternative schools, economic development projects, after-school tutorial programs, Bible studies, and athletics. Every year UrbanPromise recruits close to one hundred college-age students from around the world to volunteer a summer or year by serving some of America's neediest young people. For more information, please contact us at www.urbanpromiseusa.org.
6. Walter Brueggemann, *Genesis*, Interpretation: A Bible Commentary for Teaching and Preaching (Atlanta: John Knox Press, 1982), 315.
7. Donald T. Phillips, *Martin Luther King Jr. on Leadership* (New York: Warner Books, 1999), 319.
8. Martin Luther King Jr., "I Have a Dream," Washington, D.C., August 28, 1963.
9. Daniel Levinson, *The Seasons of a Man's Life* (New York: Ballantine Books, 1978), 98.
10. Laurent A. Parks Daloz, Cheryl H. Keen, James P. Keen, Sharon Daloz Parks, *Common Fire: Leading Lives of Commitment in a Complex World* (Boston: Beacon Press, 1996).
11. Bryant Myers, "The State of the World's Children," *The Great Commission Handbook* (1995), 80–81.
12. Gerd Theissen, *The Gospels in Context: Social and Political History in the Synoptic Tradition* (Minneapolis: Fortress, 1991), 70.
13. Judith Gundry-Volf, "Spirit, Mercy, and the Other," *Theology Today* 52, no. 1 (1995): 519.

14. Gundry-Volf, 521.
15. Matthew Barnett, *The Church That Never Sleeps* (Nashville: Thomas Nelson Publishers, 2000), 32.
16. Douglas J. Hall, *Thinking the Faith: Christian Theology in a North American Context* (Minneapolis: Fortress Press, 1991), 13.
17. Os Guinness, *The Call: Finding and Fulfilling the Central Purpose of Your Life* (Nashville: Word, 1998), 29.
18. Arthur F. Miller with William Hendricks, *Why You Can't Be Anything You Want to Be* (Grand Rapids: Zondervan Publishing House), 154.
19. Christine J. Gardner, "Tangled in the Worst of the Web," *Christianity Today*, March 5, 2001, 42–49.
20. Gardner, 46.
21. Karen A. McClintock, *Sexual Shame: An Urgent Call to Healing*, (Minneapolis: Fortress Press, 2001), 50–51.
22. Kim Hubbard, Anne-Marie O'Neill, and Christina Cheakalos, *People*, "Out of Control," April 12, 1999, 50–72.
23. Ibid., 54.
24. Ibid., 71.
25. Frederick Buechner, *Telling Secrets: A Memoir* (San Francisco: HarperSanFrancisco, 1991), 76.
26. M. Scott Peck, *The Road Less Traveled* (New York: Simon & Schuster, 1978), 53.
27. Gary Thomas, "The Forgiveness Factor," *Christianity Today*, January 10, 2000, 42.
28. Thomas, 43.
29. Frederick Buechner, *The Longing for Home: Recollections and Reflections* (San Francisco: HarperSanFrancisco, 1996), 110.
30. Ibid., 110.
31. Ibid., 111.
32. Thomas Merton quoted in "The Violence of Over-Involvement," *The Prism E-Pistle* 2, no. 21 (October 18, 2000).
33. Patricia Pearson, "Rage! We're a Culture on the Verge of Losing Control," *USA Today*, August 4, 1999, 13A.
34. Sue Klassen, "Our Sabbath Year," *Other Side*, January-February 2002, 34–35.
35. Thomas Merton, as quoted in "The Unbearable Lightness of Being Interested," *Prism*, November-December 1997, 14–15.
36. Jacques Ellul, *The Technological Bluff*, trans. Geoffrey W. Bromiley (Grand Rapids: Wm. B. Eerdmans Publishing Co., 1990), 258.
37. Tom Sine, *The Mustard Seed Conspiracy* (Waco, Texas: Word Books, 1981), 11.
38. Henri Nouwen, *Finding My Way Home: Pathways to Life and the Spirit* (Farmington, Pa.: Plough Publishing Co., 2002).
39. Mitch Albom, *Tuesdays with Morrie: An Old Man, a Young Man, and Life's Greatest Lesson* (New York: Doubleday, 1997), 124–25.

40. Ibid., 127.
41. Rabbi Shumley Boteach, Michael Segell, ed., *Hero to His Children, A Man's Journey to Simple Abundance* (New York: Scribner, 2000), 387.
42. Martin Luther King Jr., *Why We Can't Wait* (New York: Harper & Row, 1964), 89.
43. Eugene H. Peterson, *THE MESSAGE: The New Testament in Contemporary English* (Colorado Springs, Colo.: NavPress Books, 1993), 427.
44. Peterson, 428.
45. Harriet Beecher Stowe, *Uncle Tom's Cabin* (New York: M.A. Donohue & Co., 1945), 373.
46. M. Scott Peck, *The Different Drum: Community Making and Peace* (New York: Simon & Schuster, 1987), 59.
47. George Barna, "The Church of Tomorrow," *Prism,* September–October 1997, 26.
48. Barna, 26.
49. Peter Gomes, "A Word of Encouragement," *Christian Century,* November 5, 1997, 1001.
50. Jacques Ellul, *Money and Power* (Downer's Grove, Illinois: InterVarsity Press, 1984), 75.
51. Ellul, 76.
52. Ellul, 110.
53. Donald Dayton, "Recovering a Heritage: The Tappan Brothers: Business and Reform," Part 9, *Post America,* April 1975, 14–17.
54. James W. Fowler, *Weaving the New Creation: Stages of Faith and the Public Church* (San Francisco: HarperSanFrancisco, 1991), 38.
55. Fowler, 38.

Acknowledgments

Every year numerous college students sign up to work with UrbanPromise Ministries in the inner cities of Camden, New Jersey; Wilmington, Delaware; Vancouver, British Columbia; and Toronto, Ontario. These incredible young people work long hours, reside in cramped living conditions, and receive little compensation for their services—they are modern-day saints. Often, these young adults come to serve others but ultimately find themselves being transformed in the midst of loving other human beings in the name of Jesus. Watching this transformation of values, the discovery of vocation, and the deepening of faith is a life-giving gift to our ministry community and an ongoing testimony of God's keen interest in this developmental stage of human life. Thank you students!

I am grateful to our dedicated and committed staff who labor faithfully year after year, loving children and teenagers of the city unconditionally. And thanks to our board and faithful supporters—without you there would be no stories to write.

To the one who helps these stories come to life, Paul Keating, I'm indebted and thankful for your fifteen-year ministry of editing my work.

Finally, I thank my children—Calvin, Erin, and Madeline—and my wife, Pamela, for their humor, joy, and life-giving interruptions.

Please consider doing a summer or year of missionary service in the inner city with UrbanPromise. Your life will be changed forever, and you will meet some incredible children and teens. For further information or questions, please e-mail me or visit our Web page at www.urbanpromiseusa.org.